Inclusive Innovation

Innovation offers potential: to cure diseases, to better connect people, and to make the way we live and work more efficient and enjoyable. At the same time, innovation can fuel inequality, decimate livelihoods, and harm mental health. This book contends that inclusive innovation – the pursuit of innovation motivated by environmental and societal aims, with problem-owners often working with multiple stakeholders responding to challenges experienced in their local context – is able to uplift the benefits of innovation while reducing its harms.

Our approach to inclusive innovation centers around our understanding that (1) inclusion is necessarily about people and the planet, and so ecological concerns need to be at the center, (2) innovation should be understood more broadly than information technology, so that low-tech and social organization innovations are equally counted, and (3) innovation is a collaborative process in which problem-owners are crucial problem-solvers.

This book will interest researchers in the areas of development, innovation studies, and political economy.

Robyn Klingler-Vidra is Reader in Political Economy at King's College London, UK. Her research focuses on entrepreneurship, innovation, and sustainability, with a focus on East Asia. She is the author of *The Venture Capital State: The Silicon Valley Model in East Asia.*

Alex Glennie is Senior Policy Manager at the Innovation Growth Lab at Nesta, UK. Her work focuses on supporting governments to develop more inclusive and experimental innovation policies, and she has published a number of reports on the theme of inclusive innovation.

Courtney Savie Lawrence is a climate, systems, and social innovation practitioner. She has lived and worked in Asia, Africa, Europe, Latin America, and North America across the grassroots to government spectrum, including co-founding the Circular Design Lab and working with the UNDP and UNICEF innovation teams.

Routledge Studies in Innovation, Organizations and Technology

For more information about this series, please visit: www.routledge.com/
Routledge-Studies-in-Innovation-Organizations-and-Technology/book-
series/RIOT

Inclusive Innovation

Robyn Klingler-Vidra, Alex Glennie, and Courtney Savie Lawrence

Routledge
Taylor & Francis Group
LONDON AND NEW YORK

First published 2022
by Routledge
4 Park Square, Milton Park, Abingdon, Oxon OX14 4RN

and by Routledge
605 Third Avenue, New York, NY 10158

Routledge is an imprint of the Taylor & Francis Group, an informa business

British Library Cataloguing-in-Publication Data
A catalogue record for this book is available from the British Library

Library of Congress Cataloging-in-Publication Data
Names: Klingler-Vidra, Robyn, author. | Glennie, Alex, author. |
Lawrence, Courtney Savie, 1982– author.
Title: Inclusive innovation / Robyn Klingler-Vidra, Alex Glennie,
and Courtney Savie Lawrence.
Description: Milton Park, Abingdon, Oxon ; New York, NY : Routledge, 2022. |
Series: Routledge studies in innovations, organizations and technology |
Includes bibliographical references and index.
Identifiers: LCCN 2021059441 (print) | LCCN 2021059442 (ebook) |
ISBN 9780367647001 (hardback) | ISBN 9780367646998 (paperback) |
ISBN 9781003125877 (ebook)
Subjects: LCSH: Technological innovations. | Equality. | Income distribution.
Classification: LCC HC79.T4 K59977 2022 (print) |
LCC HC79.T4 (ebook) | DDC 338/.064–dc23/eng/20211214
LC record available at https://lccn.loc.gov/2021059441
LC ebook record available at https://lccn.loc.gov/2021059442

ISBN: 9780367647001 (hbk)
ISBN: 9780367646998 (pbk)
ISBN: 9781003125877 (ebk)

DOI: 10.4324/9781003125877

Typeset in Times New Roman
by Newgen Publishing UK

To the practitioners and policymakers enabling innovation that is by, and for, wider society.

Contents

Illustrations

Acknowledgments

We thank the many entrepreneurs, grassroots innovators, policymakers, practitioners, and social entrepreneurs who have shared their insights with us. Their views helped to bring the concept of inclusive innovation to life; without their stories and support, this book would not exist.

Our journey began in 2019 when we met to develop a study for the Regional Innovation Centre UNDP Asia Pacific. The study was published in March 2020 as the UNDP-Nesta *Strategies for Supporting Inclusive Innovation: insights from Southeast Asia* report. This book is an extension of that fieldwork and to the discussion and further research that it sparked. We hope to have done justice to the insights that have been shared with us. All the credit for this book's engaging content goes to our collaborators, interviewees and research assistants, while responsibility for any errors or omissions sits with us, the authors.

This book has benefited from interactions with, and support from, a number of colleagues and friends. Our academic and professional communities at King's College London, Nesta, and the United Nations Development Programme (UNDP) provided encouragement and instructive feedback throughout. Conversations, and in some cases collaborations, with colleagues, policymakers, and practitioners were essential to the book coming together. Different people wore different hats, as advisors, reviewers, lab participants, and, in some cases, direct contributors writing case studies or sharing their own compelling story. In this context, we are thankful to the following: Maesy Angelina (Pulse Lab Jakarta), Payal Arora (FemLab.Co), Stephanie Arrowsmith (Impact Hub), Omar Crespo Cardona (Link4), Amarit Charoenphan (Impact Collective), Sowirin Chuanprapun (UNESCO), Pyrou Chung (Open Development Initiative), Carolyn Curtis (TACSI), Marta Pérez Cusó (UNESCAP), Kuldeep Dantewadia (Reap Benefit), Carlo Delantar (Gobi Partners), Samuel Díaz Fernández (School of Slow Media), Xoán Fernández García (Social Innovation Consultant), Anil Gupta (Honey Bee Network), Elizabeth Hoffecker (MIT D-Lab), Kyaw Kyaw Min Htut (BEAM Education Foundation), Ishtiaque Hussain (a2i), Zainab Kakal (UNDP Fiji and the Pacific), Parkpoom Kometsopha (Reviv), Aarathi Krishnan (Berkman Klein Center at Harvard), Benjamin Kumpf (OECD), Bas Leurs

(UNDP), Julien Leyre (Future of Governance Agency), Rex Lor (UNDP Philippines), Rohan Malik (Ernst & Young), Thabiso Mashaba (These Hands), Kelly Ann McKercher (Beyond Sticky Notes), Odin Mühlenbein (Ashoka), Chris Oestereich (Linear to Circular), Elbert Or (Pushpin Visual Solutions), Jayshree Patnaik (Indian Institute of Technology), Roshan Paul (Amani Institute), Giulio Quaggiotto (UNDP SIU), Diastika Rahwidiati (Love Frankie), Karl Satinitigan (WeSolve), Adam Selzer (Civilla), Claudia Sosa Lazo (IDEO.org), Suthasiny (Moh) Sudprasert (Happy Grocers), Beenisch Tahir (UNDP Pakistan), Felicity Tan (The Rockefeller Foundation), Michou Tchana (Move92), Peerathorn Seniwong (known as P'Thorn) (Zero Baht Shop), Berlin Tran (University of Economics Ho Chi Minh City), Ida Uusikyla (UNDP Vietnam), and Liu Yan (BoP Hub). In addition, our thanks go to our advisors and collaborators on the first legs of this project. These include Hoang-Yen T. Vo (DRD Vietnam), Madeleine Gabriel (Nesta), Ye Liu (King's College London), Juliet Ollard (Nesta), Lan Phan (UNDP Vietnam), and Isaac Stanley (ex-Nesta).

Financial support provided by King's College London, including research seed funding and the King's Undergraduate Research Fellowship (KURF) schemes, enabled research assistance and the book's open access availability. Our thanks also go to the ESRC Impact Acceleration Account at King's College London for enabling interviews as part of the Voices from Vietnam research project, which revealed examples of inclusive innovation as a tool to respond to the COVID-19 pandemic in Vietnam. Our KURF research assistants, Coralie Gauvin-Belair, Elodie (Minh) Hoang, and Hanna Pham, mapped out evolving inclusive innovation activities across Southeast Asia. Nesta served as an important champion organization of our project, and this book manuscript in particular. Last, but of course not least, thank you to Yongling Lam, our editor at Routledge, for supporting our ability to write this book for the series Routledge Studies in Innovations, Organizations and Technology.

Abbreviations

AI	Artificial intelligence
ANDE	Aspen Network of Development Entrepreneurs
AR	Augmented reality
ASEAN	Association of Southeast Asian Nations
AT	Appropriate technologies
BoP	Bottom of the pyramid
CSR	Corporate social responsibility
DOST	Department of Science and Technology
DTI	Department of Trade and Industry (Philippines)
ESG	Environmental, social, and governance
FDI	Foreign direct investment
GALI	Global Accelerator Learning Initiative
GDP	Gross Domestic Product
GEF	Global Environmental Facility
GEM	Global Entrepreneurship Monitor
GIAN	Grassroots Innovation Augmentation Network
GNH	Gross National Happiness
GRIND	Grassroots Innovation for Inclusive Development
ESCAP	Economic and Social Commission for Asia and the Pacific
HCD	Human-centered design
HiFi	Hub of Innovation for Inclusion
iBoP Asia	Innovations for the Base of Pyramid
ICT	Information and communications technology
IDP	Internally displaced persons
IDRC	International Development Research Centre
IID	Innovation for Inclusive Development
ILO	International Labour Organization
IoT	Internet of Things
IR4.0	Fourth Industrial Revolution
KIC	Knowledge and Innovation Community
MARD	Ministry of Agriculture and Rural Development (Vietnam)
MOE	Ministry of Education

MOLISA	Ministries of Labour and Social Affairs (Vietnam)
MOST	Ministry of Science and Technology (Vietnam)
MOSTI	Ministry of Science, Technology and Innovation (Malaysia)
MPI	Ministry of Planning and Investment (Vietnam)
MSME	Micro-, small-, and medium-sized enterprise
NAFOSTED	National Foundation for Science and Technology Development (Vietnam)
NGO	Nongovernmental organization
NIS	National innovation systems
NXPO	National Higher Education Science Research and Innovation Policy Council (Thailand)
PRESENT	Poverty Reduction through Social Entrepreneurship (Philippines)
R&D	Research and development
RDI	Research and development institutions
RRI	Responsible research and innovation
RSI	Regional systems of innovation
SDGs	Sustainable Development Goals
SEASIN	South East Asia Social Innovation Network
SHE	Support Her Enterprise
SJI	Samdrup Jongkhar Initiative
SME	Small- and medium-sized enterprise
STEM	Science, technology, engineering, and mathematics
TBL	Triple bottom line
UN	United Nations
UNCTAD	United Nations Conference on Trade and Development
UNDP	United Nations Development Programme
UNICEF	United Nations International Children's Emergency Fund
UNIID-SEA	Universities and Councils Network on Innovation for Inclusive Development in Southeast Asia
VIIP	Vietnam Inclusive Innovation Project
VR	Virtual reality
WB	World Bank
ZBS	Zero Baht Shop

1 An introduction to inclusive innovation

Innovation offers potential: to cure diseases, to better connect people, and to make the way we live and work more efficient and enjoyable. At the same time, innovation – especially technological innovation – can fuel inequality, decimate livelihoods, and harm mental health.[1] This incongruence leads us to ask: can we uplift the benefits of innovation for the environment and society while reducing the harms? In this book, we contend that "inclusive innovation" is the form of innovation that strives to meet this ambition. We define inclusive innovation as:

> the pursuit of innovation motivated by environmental and societal aims, with problem-owners – often working with multiple stakeholders – responding to challenges experienced in their local context.

The term inclusive innovation was first used in a 2007 World Bank (WB) report, in which Mark Dutz coined the phrase in the context of sustainable innovation in India. He defined it as "knowledge creation and absorption efforts that are most relevant to the needs of the poor."[2] The emphasis for Dutz, and for many scholars and policymakers in the years since, was on social inclusion, specifically in socioeconomic terms.

We argue that the notion of innovation for environmental protection and social inclusion purposes is older than 2007. We contend that it has roots in the appropriate technologies (AT) movement that began in emerging economies in the 1960s. The AT movement aimed to assuage the tendency toward innovation investments in – and the gains being captured by – the rich, industrialized world.[3] The AT movement, epitomized by the work of Schumacher in *Small is Beautiful,* argued that innovation should be designed to leverage local inputs – particularly abundant labor – rather than replace them.[4] Instead of emerging economies inheriting technological innovations that flow from high-income to low-income consumers, Schumacher's contention was that innovation should be developed by local labor in order to solve local challenges, leverage local resources, and benefit the local environment.[5] The AT movement, as epitomized by Schumacher's thinking, advocated for small-scale, but locally-impactful, innovation, especially in developing countries.[6]

DOI: 10.4324/9781003125877-1

Despite the antecedents offered by the AT movement, inclusive innovation today frequently positions societal equality as *the* goal and high-technology as *the* solution. "Information and communications technology" (ICT) is too narrow an understanding of the techniques that can foster inclusive innovation, and socio-economic considerations too focused.[7] Given this, we argue that inclusive innovation should be understood as having (1) social processes and low-tech solutions – in addition to ICT – as essential means of driving innovation, (2) environmental concerns considered alongside societal aims, and (3) marginalized or underrepresented innovators as being able to include themselves by solving a problem that they are experiencing. Problem-owners are understood here as the affected individuals, groups, and communities themselves.

The book shares case studies and stories of inclusive innovation, primarily from across Southeast Asia. We focus on Southeast Asia for three reasons.[8] First, the region's dynamism has produced compelling examples of inclusive innovation. Second, the innovation that has fueled the region's economic growth has also increased inequality and environmental challenges.[9] Hence, there's a heightened need for innovation that addresses these challenges. Our third reason is that existing research has focused on inclusive innovation in Africa, Europe and North America. Just as the AT movement resisted the flow of technologies from the US and Europe to developing countries, so do we contend that inclusive innovation should be conceived of, and advanced, in local contexts. Thus, our focus on Southeast Asia, a dynamic, emerging region with ample need for inclusive innovation, which is understudied in terms of inclusive innovation policy and practice.

Defining inclusive innovation

We begin by defining inclusive innovation. First, let's break the term into its two parts. "*Inclusive*" refers to a feeling of belonging, of self-determination. The *Oxford English Dictionary* says simply that it is *not excluding any of the parties or groups involved in something*. Social justice activist Verna Myers explains symbolically that the difference between diversity and inclusion is one of being invited to the dance (diversity) and being asked to dance (inclusion).[10] Inclusion, then, is about a sense of belonging and an ability to participate in the decisions that shape our lives, and our lives within families, neighborhoods, and cities.

Inclusion can be in reference to many intersectional demographic characteristics, such as disability, ethnicity, gender, race, religion, or sexual-orientation. It can also be in consideration of socioeconomic position, in geographic terms, or in terms of industry and sector. To summarize, we think of inclusion broadly. It can be understood in terms of demographic traits, but also in spatial and industrial terms, and crucially, at the intersection of these different characteristics.

The other half is "innovation," which is derived from the Latin word *novus* meaning new.[11] Innovation has commonly come to be understood as the development and application of novel products or processes.[12] This includes invention, the filing of patents, and other technology-driven activity, as well as a range of social and management practices, such as new business models. Innovation, in its various incarnations, is essential to achieving economic goals including, yet not limited to, productivity gains, the growth of Gross Domestic Product (GDP) and quality of life improvements.[13] The challenge, though, is that while innovation is often considered to be a solution for many challenges facing humanity, it can also cause unintended and even negative consequences.[14]

Together, *inclusive innovation* refers to new products, or processes, that strive to improve the lives and livelihoods of problem-owners, marginalized individuals, and often excluded groups (by those actors, rather than for them). The manifestation includes boosting the more equitable distribution of economic gains, and making progress on environmental and societal challenges. There is increasing awareness of unequal rates of participation in innovation, such that women, transgender and nonconforming, ethnic minorities, differently-abled people, immigrants, and those from disadvantaged socioeconomic backgrounds are underrepresented in sectors and roles that produce and benefit from innovation.[15] To begin to remedy this inequity, inclusive innovation places problem-owners as problem-solvers, and in so doing, strives to increase participation in, and benefit from, innovation across demographic, geographic, and industrial domains.

Several terms refer to innovation that has the environment, equity, and societal missions in mind.[16] Table 1.1 alphabetically lists the definitions of these related concepts and details the associated key thinkers and publications.

In order to bring these terms together in the context of our understanding of inclusive innovation, we outline the "unjust equilibrium" that motivates each.[17] An unjust equilibrium refers to stable conditions that cause or exacerbate exclusion, marginalization, or suffering. They begin when policymakers, problem-owners or practitioners observe an injustice, one that they want to work to overhaul, toward a more just equilibrium. Given the observation of the unjust equilibrium, inclusive innovators are motivated to act in order to direct innovation attention and resources in a way that the market economy, if left to its own instincts, would not.

We emphasize the case for an understanding of inclusive innovation that places agency and contingencies at the center. Taking a Foucauldian approach to power relationships, we contend that innovators can "include themselves" rather than rely on others to include them or solve their problems. Hoffecker, in a similar way, defines inclusive innovation in the context of her research on agricultural systems as "a collaborative and co-creative multi-stakeholder approach," emphasizing agency and leadership by those traditionally excluded as central to inclusive innovation.[18] Dey and Gupta take a

Table 1.1 Related terms to inclusive innovation (listed in alphabetical order)

Term	Description and key authors
AT	A movement that emphasizes the application of technologies that are suitable to local social and economic conditions that have environmental considerations in mind and that encourage self-sufficiency on the part of those who use them.[50] Here we also include decolonial innovation[51] and place-based innovation,[52] which both emphasize fit with local context.
Assistive technologies	Describes "products or systems that support and assist individuals with disabilities, restricted mobility, or other impairments to perform functions that might otherwise be difficult or impossible."[53] Here we also note "disability justice."
Distribution-sensitive innovation	Considers distributive implications in terms of demographic, industrial, or societal dimensions.[54]
Frugal innovation	Innovative products are stripped of nonessential features in order to be made available by and for poor consumers; Prabhu defines frugal innovation as "the creation of faster, better, and cheaper solutions for more people that employ minimal resources."[55]
Grassroots innovation	Emphasizes bottom-up solutions by individuals and communities to solve local challenges. Seyfang and Smith define it as "a network of activists and organizations generating novel bottom-up solutions for sustainable development and sustainable consumption."[56] The Grassroots Innovation Augmentation Network (GIAN) defines it as "a modality of inclusive innovation that enables extremely affordable, niche-adapted solutions to local problems, often unaided by the public sector or outsiders."
Green innovation	Also called "eco-innovation," "climate innovation," or "environmental innovation." refers to "new products, processes or methods that, over the course of their life cycles, reduce environmental risks, pollution, and the negative impacts of consuming resources."[57] "Blue innovation" is a subset term, referring to innovation that targets ocean health and sustainability.
Mission-oriented innovation	A form of innovation policy that focuses on achieving a societal goal, or mission, such as reducing carbon emissions.[58] Also called "mission-driven" or "transformative" innovation as well as "tech for good."
Open innovation	Concept was popularized by Henry Chesbrough, referring to the changing dynamics whereby firms increasingly rely upon external resources and logics, and ecosystems are characterized as having greater collaboration across actors.[59]

Table 1.1 Cont.

Term	Description and key authors
Responsible research and innovation (RRI)	An approach that aims to anticipate and assess potential implications and societal expectations with regard to research and innovation. The concept was popularized in the early 2010s through the EU's framework programs, which sought to hold research to high ethical standards and ensure that policymakers took responsibility for avoiding harmful effects of innovation, including by engaging the communities affected by innovation.[60]
Rural innovation	Innovations serving farmers and people in rural areas. This form of innovation has both its demand and supply situated in its rural context.[61] The idea of "household innovation" is also included here.
Social innovation	Innovation activities that are "motivated by the goal of meeting a social need and that are predominantly developed and diffused through organizations whose primary purposes are social."[62] We mention "civic innovation" as a related term focused specifically in the context of the civil or public realm.[63]
Systems innovation	Can be considered twofold in responding or realizing an opportunity connected to a complex problem "First when society faces a systemic challenge which requires a systemic response. Second, when society has a systemic opportunity to create a new kind of system."[64] Here we also include human-centered design (HCD)[65] and "design for the pluriverse" as related concepts, and potential components of some systems innovations.[66]

similar tack by stressing that "innovations *from* grassroots are distinct from innovations *for* grassroots," in terms of their frugality, inclusivity, and sustainability.[19] Typically, grassroots innovations arise from a lack of resources and they generally address needs at the bottom of the pyramid (BoP) where formal structures or interventions are insufficient. These types of innovations are considered inclusive in that they inherently involve solutions from those who experience the challenges. They can draw on local materials or second-hand parts, and this can (but does not necessarily) offer an environmentally sustainable nature.[20]

The myriad promises of innovation have led to the development of multiple approaches that consider the social purpose of innovation, the distribution of its benefits, and the relationships of those involved. We see three motivations underlying inclusive innovation, as illustrated in Table 1.2.

The issues of direction, distribution and participation are interconnected. Some of the language used in Table 1.1 aligns with one of these core rationales, while others sit at the intersections. AT, for instance, involve both distributive

Table 1.2 Three unjust equilibria motivating inclusive innovation

	1. Participative	*2. Distributive*	*3. Directive*
Unjust equilibrium	Insufficient participation in, or benefit from, the production of innovation.	Innovation can cause – and accentuate – inequality.	Innovation, without purposeful redirection, often aims at financial – not necessarily environmental or societal – gains.
Related concepts	Frugal and grassroots innovation.	Distribution-sensitive innovation and RRI.	AI, green, grassroots, mission-oriented, systems, and social innovation.

and directive, as they advocate for innovation that is drawing on local labor and limiting environmental degradation.[21]

A brief history of inclusive innovation in Southeast Asia

Early inclusive innovation studies and initiatives in Southeast Asia emphasized the socio-economic dimension, especially in targeting BoP consumers.[22] From 2008, inclusive innovation efforts in Southeast Asia tended to center on engaging poor and rural communities. The focus on the BoP was evident in major initiatives in the region, such as the 2010 Krabi Initiative on Science, Technology and Innovation for a Competitive, Sustainable, and Inclusive ASEAN.[23] The initiative articulated a policy framework for collaboration across ASEAN and the EU that aimed to balance considerations of economic competitiveness and human development. It strived to promote innovation that included wider segments of society (i.e., youth and the BoP) as producers. Promoting inclusivity in business was articulated as a broader aim in the 2017 ASEAN Inclusive Business (IB) Framework. The ASEAN initiative applied a G20 definition of inclusive businesses as referring to businesses that

> provide goods, services, and livelihoods on a commercially viable basis, either at scale or scalable, to people at the Base of the economic Pyramid (BoP),[24] making them part of the value chain of companies' core business as suppliers, distributors, retailers or customers.[25]

Over time, the concept has been taken further, more purposefully involving people and places that are otherwise marginalized from innovation processes, and focused not just on the BoP. The emphasis, increasingly, evolved toward issues of geographic inclusion, encouraging innovation in rural areas. Recent initiatives, such as the Philippines' Inclusive Innovation Industrial Strategy and the Regional Inclusive Innovation Centers, strive for collaborative, systems-based approaches organized around bringing together a variety of individuals and organizations, such as academia, grassroots innovators, large firms, local government, small and medium-sized enterprise (SMEs), and social enterprises.[26]

Globally, the use of the phrase inclusive innovation has increased over time. Google Search Term Analytics for "inclusive innovation" from 2007 to 2020 show growth, at the world level, through 2019, and then a moderate drop in 2020. Google Search Term Analytics for each of the 11 Southeast Asian countries, though, only produced results in two countries: Malaysia and the Philippines. In Figure 1.1, we can see the significant uptake in the Philippines since 2016, and more sporadic usage of the term in Malaysia, with a spike in 2012 but then no activity until 2017 and 2018.

In large part, governments and international organizations – particularly the United Nations (UN) and World Bank – have been responsible for convening this increased interest in, and use of, inclusive innovation in select Southeast Asian countries. Governments have taken up efforts to advance

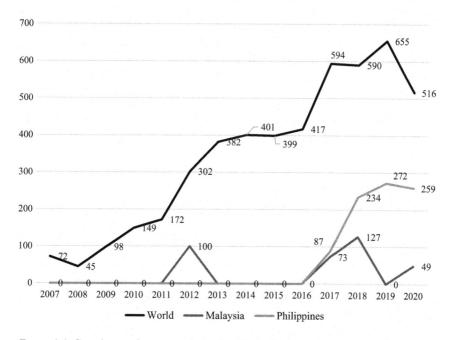

Figure 1.1 Google search term analytics for "inclusive innovation," 2007–2020

Source: Data was gathered separately for "World" and then each Southeast Asian country individually: Brunei, Cambodia, Indonesia, Laos, Malaysia, Myanmar, Philippines, Singapore, Thailand, Timor-Leste, and Vietnam. Only Malaysia and the Philippines are included in the figure because they are the only two countries that produced any results. This is, of course, not a definitive account of the use of the term (because of language issues, Google usage differences across countries, etc.), but one indicator of its prevalence and relative increase over time.

inclusive innovation through a variety of policy initiatives. As an example of an implemented policy in Southeast Asia, the Philippine Inclusive Innovation Industrial Strategy (i3S), which was first introduced in 2017 and helps explain the rise in Google results for the Philippines, encourages innovation that takes a wider view of who is conceived of as an innovator.[27] The Philippines' initiative, as well as others underway across the region, aims to bring together the whole ecosystem, so that grassroots innovators, MSMEs, universities, public research entities, and large firms collaborate to advance innovative solutions to societal challenges. The introduction of the language of inclusive innovation was specifically introduced in Malaysia through the High Impact Project 6 – Inclusive Innovation (HIP6) program, which was part of the country's SME Masterplan 2012–2020. Though Vietnam did not feature in the Google results, a similar introduction occurred there, as the World Bank launched the Vietnam Inclusive Innovation Project (VIIP) in 2013.

Since their onset, inclusive innovation policies have included initiatives that focus on the provision of different types of capital. Programs, such as the VIIP, act by directing financial capital, such as research and development (R&D) spending or startup loans, toward underrepresented groups, in an effort to increase their participation in innovation. Another brand of initiatives allocate resources toward human capital, in the form of skills training – for example, coding boot camps, or targeted provision of science, technology, engineering, and mathematics (STEM) education for women, ethnic minorities, and socioeconomically disadvantaged population groups.[28] Such provision is based on the presumption that a lack of specialized skills and experience is excluding a demographic group from work in innovative sectors; targeted computer and STEM training programs are provided to help fill the skills gap that is undermining demand from these potential applicants. As a means of boosting human capital in the form of on-the-job experience, quotas have also been set for participation, such as minimum numbers for female representation on boards or in government.

Inclusion of whom? Agency, contingencies, and problem-ownership

In our study of inclusive innovation, we begin with the "who." The "who" refers to one's feeling of belonging and openness to their involvement.[29] With this in mind, and with consideration of the social dynamics at play when we consider "participation," we acknowledge that equal starting points do not exist for individuals. Identities are fluid and intersectional, and this has an impact on how in-groups and out-groups may be conceived of in an innovation initiative. We define intersectionality here as the way "social identities such as race, class, gender, ability, geography, and age interact to form unique meanings and complex experiences within and between groups in society."[30] In conceiving of the "who", the view of in-groups and out-groups determines the bounds of "inclusion" and "exclusion." This carries with it often unseen power dynamics, which have implications on the extent to which innovation can be participatory. Thus, inclusion can be a politically loaded, nonneutral term that carries notions of power and also social equity, equality of opportunity, and democratic participation.[31]

This leads us to ask: who has agency to drive and be included in change? Whose rules of the game are to be followed, and whose interests are to be prioritized? We are particularly interested in exploring innovation that enhances livelihoods and well-being, which frequently is correlated with the ability to generate income and drive environmental regeneration. Drawing upon a development lens, Amartya Sen explains that contingencies – meaning personal circumstances such as where one is born, the extent to which they have access to resources, etc. – affect the opportunities available to them. Sen asserts, "what we can or cannot do, can or cannot achieve, does not depend just on our incomes but also on the variety of physical and social characteristics that affect our lives and make us what we are."[32] Acknowledging these distinctions helps us consider inclusive innovation in terms of the individuals, organizations, and systems involved, seeking to go beyond the "innovator as hero" narrative and also the presumption that those at the center of the social system are necessary to driving inclusion.

The hero narrative – in which a lone entrepreneur creates and implements an innovation – does not work well in the inclusive innovation domain. As Michel Foucault asserts:

> Power is everywhere: not because it embraces everything, but because it comes from everywhere. Power is not an institution, nor a structure, nor a possession. It is the name we give to a complex strategic situation in a particular society.[33]

With this in mind we explore the role of intangibles, such as relationships and their inherent power dynamics, in the context of their potential to accelerate or hinder inclusive innovation approaches. We examine means of self-empowerment, not on reliance on some central power.

Agency in inclusive innovation, then, has to do with who are the problem-owners. In inclusive innovation, problem-solvers *are often* the problem-owners. Munoz and Kimmit explain that social problems are defined and solutions are applied through social innovation that stems from, and responds to, the local context.[34] The centrality of problem-ownership and local context acknowledges the contingencies that shape one's ability to participate. Bottom-up problem-owners, often called grassroots innovators, typically operate below the radar and have driven much of the inclusive innovation in practice.[35]

The Circular Design Lab – launched in Bangkok in 2019 as a volunteer, citizen-driven open innovation "platform" – is a good example of distributed organization and self-empowerment of problem-owners as problem-solvers. It is not technically registered (the community discussed and voted against this idea), it doesn't have a director, and it doesn't have sustainable funding sources, yet it has been able to run on the energy that the ecosystem community collaboration generates. Since inception, the community has grown to over 500 members with issues addressed in "pop-up" labs. Using systemic design, action research, future design, and ethnographic tools, the community develops experiments, focused on air pollution, unsustainable fast fashion, and waste management, among other challenges that it identifies. Box 1.1 explains more about the Circular Design Lab and its inclusive approach.

Box 1.1 Circular Design Lab

By Courtney Savie Lawrence, Circular Design Lab

Launched initially as an experiment in Bangkok, Thailand, the "Circular Design Lab" is a volunteer, citizen-driven, bottom-up open innovation "platform" that focuses on tackling local environmental and social challenges leveraging a systems approach. The lab is not technically registered; the community discussed, yet voted against this idea, determining that the flat governance structure is what was part of the magic. In this sense, there is no director or a conventional organizational model. We have been able to harness microgrants for materials and volunteers for execution that have been leveraged for specific workshops, events, and ecosystem gatherings. What has been fascinating is the way the lab has been able to run on the energy that the community collaboration generates.

What brought us all together in the first place? A small group of faculty from a local university wanted to investigate the core drivers of entrenched climate and social justice issues in our own backyard of Bangkok. We were curious if others would also agree that it is our collective civic role to tackle the "badly managed commons" challenges. Our hypothesis was anchored in this question: could we curate a community of practice around tackling wicked problems from a systems perspective? Of course, we also wondered if the issues would prove too large a scale. Or would we feel too small and removed from really being able to affect change.

The Circular Design Lab now holds over 500 members, and since inception much of our work has focused on prototyping and delivering informed responses (we shy away from the language around "solution" too much) to challenges including waste management, plastics, and air pollution, as well as food and fashion supply chains – these themes are nominated and selected by the community. By working with an ecosystem approach, we often hold gatherings to connect the social capital dots. This looks like panel discussions, systemic design workshops, pop-up zero-waste happy hours and design studios. Going back to our first "lab case" where we focused on the Waste Management System in Bangkok, we had three teams collaborate to develop prototypes based on workshop-surfaced leverage points which ended up informing the ways the teams developed their experiments. One focused on mindsets, another on single-use plastic, and the third, on food waste and recycling systems. After the first lab we had significant momentum and interest so we continued! We were able to cover the cost of space and food for the workshops in the first lab thanks to a seed grant from the Royal Society of the Arts, yet for the second, we had pro-bono local support to continue – so we did – and we included lab topics as well. In the "2.0," which we held three months after the first round, we added air pollution and unsustainable fashion supply chains. The following year, in 2020, we had support from The Incubation Network to work on ocean plastic challenges as well as food systems, all in accord with our community members interests and notably issues that are problematic for Thailand too.

So how deep does the work go? Do the workshops lead to anything significant in terms of substance or the problem at hand? One example would be the "#Right2CleanAir Road Show"- which emerged from the 2.0 lab series. By partnering with the Thailand Clean Air Network, who attended the lab workshop sessions, we worked on raising awareness for political action through a series of virtual sessions and papers, including the "Clean Air Blue Paper"- an evidence-based case for policy change-which was a gap identified by the community. Throughout the road-show, which included ten online and offline sessions with simultaneous translation in English and Thai, topics including the economic cost of air pollution, its impact on various facets of life, as well as an inquiry into the gaps between current and proposed solutions. Among the outcomes of the project, certain solutions were proposed, such as cre-ative responses (arts, community and education), responses to the gaps in the system, and democratizing the access to air quality. The overall goal was to use this campaign to drive people to act – and the mech-anism to engage with was signing the citizen driven policy mechanism to table the first Clean Air Act to Parliament. Interestingly, in Thailand's legal code, with over 10,000 citizen signatures such legislation proposals can be reviewed and potentially adopted by the government. At the time of writing there are nearly 25,000 and counting.

For readers curious about process, although we are always evolving the approach (and arguably, COVID-19 required that rethink), at a high level, we facilitate a systemic design approach to surface points that tackle such complex issues. It begins by having groups work together to gather information regarding the specific problem and its context. We call this co-initializing as it enables individuals to learn from diverse perspectives and discover the challenges and opportunities that can be observed in this field, often through action research and ethnography. Then, co-sensing takes place, where groups assess the data and investigate the driving forces behind these complex issues and start identifying the core drivers and potential leverage points to intervene. We hold space to 'make sense' of the collected data and re-imagine what might be possible instead, framing problem statements in the meantime. Third, co-creation. This is the stage where the groups foster, test, and refine the ideas they developed in the two previous stages. They produce prototypes to test locally. Fourth, the co-evolution stage takes place. Stories are shared, including the experiences of each group member where reflection on how they experienced the process and what they learned is critical. The circle is often expanded organically as new connections are made, and previous ones are deepened.

As the Circular Design Lab case shows, systems-based inclusive innovation initiatives require decisions about how to structure the organization, and these decisions affect the nature of hierarchy and inclusion. In addition to questions about how to structure, power dynamics potentially resurface when the problem-owners are not engaged. The innovation space is full of co-creation and co-consensus processes, yet there is a danger to these methods if the actors engage only with understandings and contexts that fit with their own intention.[36] In an effort to avoid this pitfall, the Circular Design Lab participants explain that "the goal is to build relevant testing grounds that usher in opportunity spaces, or eventual interventions to shock the system to shift in a new direction." One of their prototypes has led to the co-championing of the country's first citizen-driven Clean Air Act – a bottom-up policy process that leads to legislation being tabled at the Thai Parliament. Examples such as the Circular Design Lab respond to the question of who owns "problems" in an inclusive way.

People and planet: ecological integration

Power dynamics and who should, or who can, own the problem is more complex given the centrality of environmental concerns at the core of our understanding of inclusive innovation. In the so-called current "Decade of Action," the race to accelerate solutions toward the UN Sustainable Development Goals (SDGs) by 2030, there is little questioning the importance of innovation for climate and the environment. Human activity is linked to driving the world's sixth mass extinction with overpopulation, consumption of resources, and doubling of emissions threatening all corners of the globe.[37] Take, for example, the Philippines, which is vulnerable to the impact of climate change owing to its proximity to the Pacific Ocean's typhoon belt and environmental degradation.[38] This manifests as exposure to flooding or droughts, public health risks, threats to biodiversity and food security, loss of livelihoods and human life, among others.

For now, though, there is still focus on people first and the environment second. One of the core challenges, we contend, is to focus on regenerative development, sustainability, and the environment as central to inclusive innovation. This requires a shift away from one where science traditionally siloes human and ecological issues as independent issues[39] and returns toward one that sees the environment and society as interdependent, as indigenous and traditional ecological knowledge have done for hundreds of years.[40] In practice, there are already nature-based innovative solutions evolving, which Cohen-Shacham and co-authors define as actions that are "simultaneously providing human well-being and biodiversity benefits."[41]

The reframe of inclusive innovation – toward people and planet, rather than only social concerns – is challenging given the multiple tragedies-of-the-commons dilemmas.[42] Tragedy-of-the-commons refers to the tendency for a limited (public) resource, such as the oceans or air, being depleted, as no one person feels responsible for maintaining it or limiting their use. The challenge is that many believe that if others reduce their pollution, or their consumption, the crisis could be averted. As Kate Raworth argues in her book *Doughnut Economics: Seven Ways to Think Like a 21st-Century Economist*, the answer involves shifting our thinking so that we stay within the planetary boundaries, or "doughnut," which she conceives of as a social boundary in relation to ecological capacity.[43] The doughnut is based on principles of circular design and use, reducing consumption, and becoming more regenerative in order to operate within the boundary.

An example of green innovation that has societal implications is the Liter of Light initiative, which began in the Philippines. The Liter of Light began in places such as remote islands, where electricity grids do not fully reach all communities and houses, and in those on the grid, where brownouts occur frequently. The insecure access to electricity left residents without light and, as such, they either need to be outdoors, in the heat and sun, or inside, in the dark. At the same time, the creators of Liter of Light noticed that there was significant waste caused by single-use plastics, particularly bottles. Plastic bottles, in some places, were littering towns and waterways. These two disparate problems – insufficient access to energy and environmental degradation due to plastic waste – are the issues that Liter of Light solves.

The Liter of Light innovation solves the problems by taking every day plastic bottles and cleaning them, and filling them with water and chlorine. The bottles are then inserted into a circular hole on the roof of a home. When the sun shines, the mild chemical reaction in the bottle creates usable light on the inside of the building. This means that electricity cables, or generators, are not needed and plastic waste is reduced and infused with new purpose. More than that, a new brand of "green jobs" has been created around the installation of the liters. So, the Liter of Light innovation offers an inexpensive, and low-tech, solution to the problems of insufficient indoor light and plastic waste.

Liter of Light is similar to other initiatives in its twin aims, as a growing number of inclusive innovations provide better conditions for both people and the planet. Take, for example, Gaz Lite, a liquefied petroleum gas canister developed by Filipino firm PR Gaz to solve the problem of indoor air pollution from the use of solid fuels such as wood and charcoal. Benefits are multifaceted: the canisters offer better health, shorter cooking times, lower household expenses, and micro-entrepreneurship opportunities (PR Gaz has set up over 800 community stores as canister retailers).

Another example of waste reduction, environmental regeneration, and livelihood gains is Pasar Sejahtera, based in Indonesia. Pasar Sejahtera (translation means "prosperous market") aims to improve pasar (markets) as physical spaces, in order to encourage more local people to shop there rather than in modern supermarkets (which are less tied into the local economy and community). This is achieved by innovating waste management processes, in the form of inorganic "waste banks" and composting facilities, which help markets meet hygiene standards and provide financial opportunities for traders. Locals receive cash in return for waste they deliver to the banks, which they can then use to build their business. Other measures include the formation of trader and laborer cooperatives, and education on financial literacy, health, and sustainability.[44]

The potential scale of engagement with Pasar Sejahtera is sizable: 12 million people in Indonesia rely directly on traditional markets for their income, with 50 million (almost a fifth of the population) relying on them indirectly. This makes the sector the second biggest in terms of employment after agriculture. Efforts to improve livelihoods here thus have the potential to bring great benefit to a significant number of households. Reflecting the importance of the initiative, President Joko Widodo identified traditional markets as a part of his Nawacita ("nine-point") development program for Indonesia in 2014. This election pledge has been developed into a national market revitalization program (Revitalisasi Pasar Rakyat), launched by the Ministry of Trade in 2015 with the aim of developing 5,000 such markets across Indonesia.

Our inclusive innovation framework

Our inclusive innovation framework centers around the understanding that (1) inclusion is necessarily about people *and* the planet, and so ecological concerns need to be at the center, (2) innovation should be understood more broadly than information technology, so that low-tech and social organization innovations are equally counted, and (3) innovation is a collaborative process in which problem-owners are crucial problem-solvers.

We study inclusive innovation by focusing on the questions underpinning the source and the means of innovation, in terms of their *how, what,* and *where*. For us, as discussed in the previous section, the "who" is understood as the problem-owner and is at the center of any initiative. The "why" of inclusive innovation, as with the related terms we canvassed, has to do with the observation of an unjust equilibrium; the desire to address a locally-experienced environmental and social challenge. Knowing the "who" and "why", our framework turns to examining inclusive innovation according to its how, what, and where.

1. **How: innovation by and for problem-owners** aims to enhance the quality of life and work in local communities, regions and sectors experiencing challenges. Initiatives might seek to improve institutions, processes and workplace technologies toward greater productivity and higher incomes, or upgrade the infrastructure of people's daily lives in order to enable an improved experience (be that via access to employment, or through better health). These innovations are characterized by their enabling effect, in that they provide better conditions by and for marginalized or resource-scarce groups. It also constitutes social innovations – or creative, collaborative and process-based solutions – to societal challenges.

2. **What: innovation for environmental and social good** involves the development of technology-based solutions to address social or environmental challenges such as waste collection, education provision, low incomes in the agricultural sector, or infrastructure issues facing excluded groups. In line with the antecedents to inclusive innovation – particularly AT – we focus on technology as broader than information and communications technology and a key medium for helping to ameliorate complex challenges. Consumers of these types of innovations receive products and services that are affordable and tailored to their needs and circumstances, improved market access, and enhanced opportunities to use innovative approaches and tools that can boost their incomes.

3. **Where: innovation everywhere** refers to interventions where innovative activities are intended to be further geographically distributed, both in their development and in their application. This approach sees innovation as an economic and social process, designed to broaden access in spatial terms. It offers, in principle, a systematic means of creating regionally spread development and greater shared prosperity, typically to rural, mountainous, or socioeconomically disadvantaged areas (including in urban settings).

This delineation of dimensions according to how, what, and where is akin to Schillo and Robinson's mapping of inclusive innovation in developed country contexts in terms of the "big five" questions.[45] Figure 1.2 offers a visual summary of the three domains of our framework.

Figure 1.2 Our inclusive innovation framework
Source: Visualized by Pushpin Visual Solutions.

To help operationalize these approaches, Table 1.3 distills each into their rationale, target issue, or group, and links them to the related concepts.

The rationale for acting and determining whether efforts are focusing on the how, what, or where are central to our framework. Stemming from this, we detail the target issues or groups for the efforts. In this way, the "rationale" is akin to frameworks that emphasize direction, participation, and governance.[46] The "related concepts" column helps us to connect the activities with other concepts discussed.

As the table shows, there is overlap across target issues and groups as well as the related terms. This overlap represents the intersectional nature of the issues addressed, similar to the way that Planes-Satorra and Paunov conceive of industrial, social, and territorial types as interrelated forms of inclusive innovation.[47] For example, grassroots innovation can manifest in each of the types, depending on whether the emphasis is on the technological medium, on solving environmental challenges encountered by rural, or disconnected populations (such as the remote islands in the Philippines which we illustrate in Chapter 4), or solutions developed by low-income communities as a means of reducing waste.

Table 1.3 Our inclusive innovation framework: how, what, where

	Rationale	Target issues or groups	Related concepts
1. How: innovation by and for problem-owners	The process of innovation should be inclusive, by problem-owners, often in collaboration with multiple stakeholders, rather than heropreneurs acting alone to address others' challenges.	• Climate change and related vulnerabilities. • Disadvantaged socioeconomic areas and groups. • Environmental degradation. • Low-income individuals. • People with disabilities.	• Assistive technologies. • Barefoot entrepreneur. • BoP. • Frugal innovation. • Grassroots innovation. • Green innovation. • Mission-oriented innovation. • Open innovation. • RRI. • Social innovation. • Systems innovation.
2. What: innovation for environmental and social good	Technology-based solutions can exacerbate inequality and exclusion, but also ameliorate inequality and drive environmental benefits.	• Increase participation of underrepresented demographic groups. • Advance the productivity of low-tech sectors. • Rural and disconnected areas.	• Assistive technologies. • Appropriate technologies. • Green innovation. • Mission-oriented innovation. • RRI.
3. Where: innovation everywhere	Innovation needs greater spatial reach, in terms of where it occurs, in order to address challenges in rural and urban arenas.	• Climate change and related vulnerabilities. • Low-income or low-productivity areas. • Rural and mountainous regions.	• Distribution-sensitive innovation. • Grassroots innovation. • Green innovation. • Place-based innovation. • Rural innovation. • Social innovation.

Data and methods

The book's analysis draws on three sets of inputs. First, interviews with more than 50 practitioners and policymakers were conducted across the region, which included (pre-COVID-19) interviews across Southeast Asia in August and September 2019. These interviews provided us with rich insights that we hand-coded in order to identify emerging themes and patterns. The coding of interview data helped us to develop our initial understanding of various approaches to inclusive innovation in emerging market contexts, especially in Southeast Asia.

Second, in order to develop a comprehensive understanding of contemporary practice, we compiled a novel dataset of inclusive innovators operating across all 11 countries in Southeast Asia: Brunei, Cambodia, Indonesia, Laos, Malaysia, Myanmar, Philippines, Singapore, Thailand, Timor-Leste, and Vietnam. To identify the inclusive innovators, we developed a set of inclusive innovation keywords (our "dictionary"), as identified in our literature review and through our interview data. We combined different terms from the dictionary – along with country names – to create the following search strings:

- Innovation / entrepreneur / technology.
- Inclusion / inclusive / inclusivity / participation / underrepresented / participate / employment / job / work / consumer / producer / underserved / livelihood.
- Grassroots / social enterprise / civil society / community / startup / policy / initiative / government.
- Poverty / poor / disadvantaged / marginalized / low-income / unbanked.
- Gender / women / girls / race / ethnicity / ethnic minority / indigenous / age / youth / elderly / limited mobility / disabled people / amputee / sex worker.
- Traditional / handicraft / artisan / fisher / farmer / grower / rural / remote.
- Sustainable / sustainability / environment / green technology / climate change / SDG / waste / upcycling / recycling / circular / pollution.
- Social challenge / societal challenge / SDG / mission / purpose.

Searches combining these keywords into strings were conducted on Google in both English and in local languages in each country. Finally, these searches led us to identify specific organizations, and also led us to accelerators and incubators focused on inclusive innovation. When our search strings helped us find one of these types of initiatives, or entrepreneurship support organizations, we scanned it with a view to then include its participants in our list. We included a number of such inclusive innovation support organizations, including the Social Venture Lab at the National University of Singapore and the Youth Co-Labs run by UNDP across the region.

Results were then hand-coded for their organization type: (1) grassroots innovator, (2) MSME / SME, (3) startup, (4) funder / investor, (5) large firm,

(6) civil society or community organization, and (7) government / international organization.[48] Each qualifying organization – across these seven types – was added to our dataset, and further details coded. We gathered the name(s) of the founders or executives, their gender, title, professional biography, country, social media details (Twitter, Facebook, LinkedIn), and organization websites. Gathering these details ensured that we had a variety of voices according to the country, organization type, etc. Once the database was complete, we then shared it with ecosystem support organizations and champions (nodes and networks themselves) across Southeast Asia, to ask for their additional recommendations and critique. This led to the identification of more contacts working across countries in the region, as well as interesting conversations about how to qualify, or in some cases disqualify, an entry.

In total, the dataset was finalized with a total of 199 Southeast Asian inclusive innovation ecosystem entries. We coded each individual (those who champion and/or implement inclusive innovation whom we refer to going forward as an "innovator") for the type of inclusive innovation to which their efforts were most closely aligned: "how," "what," or "where." In addition, each coder provided a rationale as to why this coding decision was made. Some organizations had multiple types coded, reflecting the intersectional nature of its aims and activities. This helped in three ways. First, it produced a more systematic sense of the orientation of a variety of inclusive innovation efforts. This helped us to understand if there were inclusive innovators primarily focused on one type more than the others. Second, it gave us another chance to test our typology, to see how it could be applied to nearly 200 inclusive innovators. Third, and more tactically, it helped to inform the way we organized the distribution of case studies and stories throughout the book.

Our third data source stems from a series of (Zoom-based) Inclusive Innovation Stories and Learning Labs that we led between April and June 2021 to gather insights into the practice of inclusive innovation from across South and Southeast Asia. In addition to sharing their stories directly, the labs also helped us to test and validate the themes that emerged through the two other stages. The Labs had a total of 35 participants that resulted in 7 stories and 20 case studies. In addition, we collaborated with a Philippines-based visual note-taking firm (Pushpin Visual Solutions), who helped us distil key insights from each story and from the lab plenary discussions. With these stories, included as "call-out boxes" in the authors' own voices, we create space to hear directly from a variety of people who are advancing inclusive innovation. And, through their stories, we aim to bring the subject together – and to life – for the reader.

It is important to us to ensure that our findings resonate with those *doing* inclusive innovation. So, over the course of the project we presented our findings, and had ongoing conversations, with our burgeoning inclusive innovation community. This includes the participants in our stories labs, and our interviewees, and also our wider Inclusive Innovation Community of

Practice on LinkedIn. In the early days of the project, we presented our conceptualization of inclusive innovation and the three emerging types in several action-oriented research sessions in the region. This includes the ASEAN-China-UNDP 2019 Symposium: Innovation in Achieving the SDGs and Eradicating Poverty, held in September 2019, with policymakers and inclusive innovators from across the region in attendance who also shared their reactions to our emerging typologies. We gathered their feedback through Mentimeter polls (conducted in real time) and large-print posters, which the attendees worked on in roundtable groups during the session. Our evolving understanding of the rationale and target issues benefited a great deal from this early input.

The first question we asked was "what words or phrases do you associate with 'inclusive innovation' (without using the words 'inclusive' or 'innovation')?" Out of 61 respondents the top key words and phrases that emerged were *participatory, equality, power dynamics, transformative*, and *leave no one behind*. There was a range of terms used, as Figure 1.3 shows.

The second question we asked was, "Which of the three dimensions of Inclusive Innovation (direction, participation, or governance) in the framework is most significant in your context?" The follow-up question was, "Why do you think this dimension of inclusive innovation is most significant in your context?" One of the most prominent themes that emerged in the 25 responses received was the idea that inclusive innovation needs to focus on genuinely being inclusive. The understanding of "who" to include focused on the vulnerable and marginalized, those living in poverty, rural farmers, and youth. Several respondents mentioned how important it is to consider power

Figure 1.3 ASEAN Symposium (2019) inclusive innovation word cloud
Source: Author's image from Mentimeter.
Note: Size and centrality reflect the frequency of words' mentions.

dynamics and the need to accompany rhetoric with action, so that inclusive innovation is not simply a buzzword.

In addition, there was consensus that the role of actors involved in inclusive innovation is critical. It was essential, according to the participants, to engage "as many stakeholders as possible from all sectors of society" in order to "identify a set of well-researched user needs." Governance and policy were also named as effective methods for launching inclusive innovation, but the most difficult to practice; "democratizing access" to inclusive innovation was another concern raised. Avoiding an "inclusive gap" and having "innovation as a mindset" were several pieces of guidance given to quell concerns. Overall, an overlapping theme that emerged was ensuring that it wasn't just innovation taking place, but that it was inclusive, participatory, and had a visible impact.

The third question in the poll was, "What is the best example of Inclusive Innovation you can think of in your context?" The wide range of answers given could be organized into two categories: (1) providing marginalized groups with skills/training, or (2) innovative technology. In terms of marginalized groups, there were mentions of participatory design labs, training, and skills workshops specifically for women. The second category, technology-based inclusive innovation, included solutions such as mobile banking, financial inclusion programs, and mobile markets for ethnic minority groups. There was also the theme of changing entire systems, including social security, so that it would be inclusive of those in rural areas and provide equal protection regardless of geographic location.

We then received feedback on the initial typology through the UNDP-Nesta (online) report launch event in March 2020, and the ensuing one-to-one discussions with various stakeholders afterwards. Finally, we began each of the Learning and Stories Labs (between April and June 2021) by outlining our inclusive innovation framework, and asking participants to reflect on if, and how, their own experiences align with the typologies.

As we worked with our storytellers, our understanding of the three types – and how they have been evolving in light of the COVID-19 pandemic – necessarily evolved and deepened. The time period for data collection and story development was longer, and more digital, than we had originally anticipated. In the end, we are grateful for this additional time as it has given us an opportunity to glean the perspective of more storytellers and stakeholders in higher fidelity and enriched our understanding of the rationale and operations of inclusive innovators across the region. In particular, the book now reflects the inspiring ways in which inclusive innovation is bolstering the response to the COVID-19 pandemic and the centrality of empowering problem-owners as problem-solvers.

How the book is organized

There are five chapters and we have written the book so that you can read them in any order, focusing on stories and themes that you are interested in. Chapters 2 through 4 are thematically-organized, offering stories and concepts-in-practice from across the region, according to the following three approaches to inclusive innovation:

- How: innovation by and for problem-owners.
- What: innovation for environmental and social good.
- Where: innovation everywhere.

Each chapter includes stories to bring inclusive innovation to live and to distil the ways in which inclusive innovation has evolved. The chapters are organized in sections that answer key questions in terms of how, what, and where; we then close each chapter with a section which breaks down (a) who is involved, and how, as well as (b) strengths and shortcomings. In each chapter, the "who is involved" is covered in order of Academia, Civil society, Funders and investors, Government and international organizations, Grassroots innovators, Large firms, Startups and SMEs. The stories show how inclusive innovation is not a linear journey; as they illustrate, there are wins, personal challenges, and many points for pivots and learning. We hope that these stories help to show you the reality of inclusive innovation in a way that is honest and inspiring.

In Chapter 5 we draw together the theory, policy, and practice of the future of inclusive innovation. It has been our experience throughout fieldwork, labs, and presentations that the lack of a shared language is an issue that has undermined the ability for those doing inclusive innovation, and those writing about it, and designing policy to enable it, to come together. To help foster a common understanding, the final chapter distils key debates and conceptual understandings in the language of inclusive innovation. We explore the future of inclusive innovation, especially in the post COVID-19 pandemic context, and also offer a horizon scan of what is to come in the future of inclusive innovation. This means reimagining how the notion of inclusive innovation can be further fit for future purpose.

Throughout the book, our key themes will appear. First, that inclusive innovation needs to consider people *and* the planet. The emphasis of inclusive innovation in recent years has been focused more on people, initially in terms of the BoP, and then other demographic traits. Our contention is that inclusion is fundamentally an intersectional notion; we cannot fully address societal challenges – especially in a distributive sense – if we are not integrating ecological considerations. Second, we advocate for an understanding of inclusive innovation that sees technology as an enabler for delivery of environmentally and socially good outcomes, rather than an end in itself. We see inclusive innovation as going "beyond Silicon Valley"[49] in placing people and the planet first, and drawing on a wide range of technologies, rather than information and communications technology, as the AT movement did. Third, drawing on a Foucauldian understanding of power relations, we assert the need for inclusive innovation to emphasize problem-owners as crucial problem-solvers.

Inclusion is not to be done by someone else, but rather, inclusive innovation is by, and for, oneself.

Notes

1 Elena Martellozzo, "Life is digital by default – so what's the impact on young people's mental health?" LSE Blog, December 21, 2020. https://blogs.lse.ac.uk/medialse/2020/12/21/life-is-digital-by-default-so-whats-the-impact-on-young-peoples-mental-health/; Rainer Kattel and Mariana Mazzucato, "Mission-oriented innovation policy and dynamic capabilities in the public sector." *Industrial and Corporate Change* 27, no. 5 (2018): 787–801; Susan Cozzens and Dhanaraj Thakur, *Innovation and Inequality Emerging Technologies in an Unequal World* (London: Edward Elgar, 2014); William Lazonick and Mariana Mazzucato, "The risk-reward nexus in the innovation-inequality relationship: who takes the risks? Who gets the rewards?" *Industrial and Corporate Change* 22, no. 4 (2013): 1093–1128.
2 Mark A. Dutz, *Unleashing India's Innovation: Toward Sustainable and Inclusive Growth* (Washington, DC: World Bank, 2007), xv.
3 Carroll Pursell, "The rise and fall of the appropriate technology movement in the United States, 1965–1985." *Technology and Culture*, 34, no. 3 (1993): 629–637; Nicolas Jequier, *Appropriate Technology: Problems and Promises* (Paris: OECD Development Center, 1976); David Dickson, *Alternative Technology and the Politics of Technical Change* (London: Fontana/Collins, 1974).
4 E.F. Schumacher, *Small Is Beautiful: A Study of Economics As If People Mattered* (London: Vintage (1973) [1993]).
5 Raphael Kaplinsky, "Schumacher meets Schumpeter: appropriate technology below the radar." *Research Policy* 40, no. 2 (2011): 193–203.
6 Joanna Chataway, Rebecca Hanlin, and Raphael Kaplinsky, "Inclusive innovation: an architecture for policy development." *Innovation and Development* 4, no. 1 (2014): 33–54; Cozzens and Thakur, *Innovation and Inequality Emerging Technologies in an Unequal World.*
7 We strive to show that ICT is just one means of innovation; technological innovation should, we contend, be considered in terms of its broader meaning of the term as a craft or skill, rather than only constituting high-tech or computer-related forms.
8 As researchers currently based in Europe, our ability to conduct this research has benefited from our partnerships and openness to those active in, and studying, inclusive innovation in Southeast Asia. Without their support, we would not have access to what is happening on the ground. Our sincere thanks – once again – to all those who took the time to speak to us and share their experiences and perspectives.
9 See Amartya Sen, "From income inequality to economic inequality." *Southern Economic Journal* 64, no. 2, (1997): 384–401.
10 Verna Myers, "Diversity doesn't stick without inclusion." February 4, 2017. www.vernamyers.com. May 17, 2021. www.vernamyers.com/2017/02/04/diversity-doesnt-stick-without-inclusion/.
11 Jack Springman, "Drop innovation from your vocabulary." *Harvard Business Review.* September 15, 2011. https://hbr.org/2011/09/drop-innovation-from-your-voca.

12 Peter Drucker, *Innovation and Entrepreneurship* (New York: Harper & Row, 1985); Joseph A. Schumpeter, *The Theory of Economic Development: An Inquiry into Profits, Capital, Credit, Interest and the Business Cycle* (New York: Oxford University Press, 1934); Joseph A. Schumpeter, *Capitalism, Socialism and Democracy* (New York: Harper Press, 1942).

13 Philippe Aghion, Celine Antonin, and Simon Bunel, *The Power of Creative Destruction: Economic Upheaval and the Wealth of Nations* (Cambridge, MA: Belknap Press of Harvard University Press, 2021).

14 Nitin Nohria and Hemant Taneja, "Managing the unintended consequences of your innovations." *Harvard Business Review.* January 19, 2021; J.J. Voeten and W.A. Naudé, "Regulating the negative externalities of enterprise cluster innovations: lessons from Vietnam." *Innovation and Development* 4, no. 2 (2014): 203–219.

15 Robyn Klingler-Vidra and Ye Liu, "Inclusive innovation policy as social capital accumulation strategy." *International Affairs*, 96, no. 4, (2020): 1033–1050.

16 Other works on inclusive innovation have also engaged with related terms. For instance, in the following works, the authors speak of grassroots innovation, frugal innovation, and inclusive user-producer interactions: Richard Heeks, Christopher Foster, and Yanuar Nugroho, "New models of inclusive innovation for development." *Innovation and Development* 4, no. 2 (2014): 175–185; Richard Heeks, Christopher Foster, and Yanuar Nugroho, *New Models of Inclusive Innovation for Development* (London: Routledge, 2015).

17 Roger L. Martin and Sally Osberg, "Social entrepreneurship: the case for definition." *Stanford Social Innovation Review.* Spring (2007): 29–39.

18 Elizabeth Hoffecker, "Understanding inclusive innovation processes in agricultural systems: a middle-range conceptual model." *World Development* 140 (2021): 105382.

19 Anamika Dey and Anil Gupta, "Policies and strategies to promote grassroots innovation workbook." *UNESCAP* August (2020): 5.

20 For more on the relationship between frugal innovation, AT, and sustainability, see Martin Albert, "Sustainable frugal innovation: the connection between frugal innovation and sustainability." *Journal of Cleaner Production*, 237, no. 2 (2019): 117747; Eugenia Rosca, Jack Reedy, and Julia C. Bendul, "Does frugal innovation enable sustainable development? A systematic literature review." *The European Journal of Development Research* 30 (2018): 136–157; Catherine P. Bishop, "Sustainability lessons from appropriate technology." *Current Opinion in Environmental Sustainability* 49 (2021) 50–56. Across this and related scholarship, there is a debate about the positive implications of AT for both the environment and society, with scholars finding that there are unintended negative consequences.

21 Pursell, "The rise and fall of the appropriate technology movement"; Kaplinsky, "Schumacher meets Schumpeter."

22 Christopher Foster and Richard Heeks, "Conceptualizing inclusive innovation: modifying systems of innovation frameworks to understand diffusion of new technology to low-income consumers." *European Journal of Development Research* 25 no. 3 (2013): 333–355.

23 ASEAN refers to the Association of Southeast Asian Nations.

24 For a review of the literature on the BoP, see Krzysztof Dembek, Nagaraj Sivasubramaniam, and Danielle A. Chmielewski, "A systematic review of the

bottom/base of the pyramid literature: cumulative evidence and future directions." *Journal of Business Ethics* 165 no. 3 (2020): 365–382.

25 ASEAN, *ASEAN Inclusive Business Framework.* August 14, 2017. https://asean.org/wp-content/uploads/2012/05/ASEAN-Inclusive-Business-Framework.pdf. 2.

26 "Inclusive innovation industrial strategy." Department of Trade and Industry, Government of Philippines. October 4, 2021. http://innovate.dti.gov.ph/resources/i3s-strategy/inclusive-innovation-industrial-strategy/.

27 "Inclusive innovation industrial strategy." Department of Trade and Industry, Government of Philippines. October 4, 2021. http://innovate.dti.gov.ph/resources/i3s-strategy/inclusive-innovation-industrial-strategy/.

28 Robyn Klingler-Vidra, *Global Review of Diversity and Inclusion in Business Innovation* (London: LSE Consulting and Innovate UK, 2019).

29 Myers, "Diversity doesn't stick without inclusion."

30 Olena Hankivsky and Renee Cormier, "Intersectionality and public policy: some lessons from existing models." *Political Research Quarterly* 64, no. 1 (2010): 217.

31 Theo Papaioannou, "How inclusive can innovation and development be in the twenty-first century?" *Innovation and Development* 4, no. 2 (2014): 187–202.

32 Amartya Sen, *Inequality Reexamined* (Oxford: Clarendon Press, 1992).

33 Michael Foucault, *Histoire de la sexualité* (Paris: Gallimard, 1976), 93.

34 Jonathan Kimmitt and Pablo Munoz, "Re-thinking the ethics of inclusive innovation." *International Social Innovation Research Conference,* September 2015.

35 Chataway, Hanlin, and Kaplinsky, "Inclusive innovation."

36 Soren Vestor Haldrup, "We are experimenting with different approaches to systems transformation – here are five insights." *UNDP Innovation.* May 14, 2021. https://medium.com/@undp.innovation/we-have-experimented-with-different-approaches-to-systems-transformation-here-are-five-insights-ae545a2339b1.

37 IPBES, *Global Assessment Report on Biodiversity and Ecosystem Services of the Intergovernmental Science-Policy Platform on Biodiversity and Ecosystem Services,* E.S. Brondizio, J. Settele, S. Díaz, and H.T. Ngo (ed), IPBES secretariat, Bonn, Germany, 2019; Gerardo Ceballos, Paul H. Ehrlich, and Rodolfo Dirzo, "Biological annihilation via the ongoing sixth mass extinction signaled by vertebrate population losses and declines." *Proceedings of the National Academy of Sciences* 114, no. 30 (2017): E6089–E6096.

38 Max Fisher, "This map shows why the Philippines is so vulnerable to climate change." *Washington Post.* November 12, 2013.

39 Symma Finn, Mose Herne, and Dorothy Castille, "The value of traditional ecological knowledge for the environmental health sciences and biomedical research." *Environmental Health Perspectives* 125, no. 8 (2017): 085006.

40 Shanley Knox and Felicity Tan, "For regenerative impact, social entrepreneurs must first become system entrepreneurs." *Journal of Regenerative Theory and Practice* (2021): 1–7.

41 Emmanuelle Cohen-Shacham, Gretchen Walters, C. Janzen, and Stewart Maginnis (eds) *Nature-Based Solutions to Address Global Societal Challenges* (Gland, Switzerland: IUCN, 2016), xii.

42 Mark Van Vugt, "Averting the tragedy of the commons: using social psychological science to protect the environment. Current directions in psychological science." *Current Directions in Psychological Science* 18, no. 3 (2009): 169–173.

43 Kate Raworth, *Doughnut Economics: Seven Ways to Think Like a 21st-Century Economist* (New York: Random House, 2017).

44 The Pasar Sejahtera program is funded and delivered by independent foundation Yayasan Danamon Peduli (YDP) in partnership with the Ministry of Health and the Ministry of Trade, and has been running since 2010 in 13 sites across Indonesia. Both ministries had previously been involved with pasar in limited capacities, but local government funding for development was very low. YDP provides initial funding and advice on financial infrastructure elements such as waste banks and cooperatives, while Ministries provide training in their areas of expertise. Ministry of Health involvement also includes a mandatory clinic within the market space, and a radio station informing market users on health matters.

45 R. Sandra Schillo and Ryan M. Robinson, "Inclusive innovation in developed countries: the who, what, why, and how." *Technology Innovation Management Review* 7, no. 7 (2017): 34–46.

46 The "direction, participation and governance" rubrics are central to Nesta's work on inclusive innovation. See Isaac Stanley, Alex Glennie, and Madeleine Gabriel, "How inclusive is innovation policy? Insights from an international comparison" (London: Nesta, 2018). Also, Alex Glennie, Isaac Stanley, Juliet Ollard, and Robyn Klingler-Vidra, "Strategies for supporting inclusive innovation" (London: Nesta and UNDP, 2020). Schillo and Robinson, "Inclusive innovation in developed countries" uses similar language, specifically participation, processes, outcomes, and governance.

47 Sandra Planes-Satorra and Caroline Paunov, "Inclusive innovation policies: lessons from international case studies." OECD Science, Technology and Industry Working Papers, 2017/02 (Paris: OECD, 2017).

48 The distinction between large firm and SMEs was made on the basis that enterprises can be classified into different categories according to their size; for this purpose, different criteria may be used, but the most common is the number of people employed. SMEs employ fewer than 250 people. SMEs are further subdivided into micro enterprises (fewer than 10 employees), small enterprises (10–49 employees), and medium-sized enterprises (50–249 employees). Large enterprises employ 250 or more people.

49 Robyn Klingler-Vidra, *Beyond Silicon Valley: An Inclusive Innovation Model for Southeast Asia* (Bangkok: Regional Innovation Centre UNDP Asia Pacific, 2019).

50 Schumacher, *Small Is Beautiful*; Dickson, *Alternative Technology*; Jequier, *Appropriate Technology*; Kaplinsky, "Schumacher meets Schumpeter."

51 Michael Dominguez, "Decolonial innovation in teacher development: praxis beyond the colonial zero-point." *Journal of Education for Teaching* 45, no. 1 (2019): 47–62.

52 Philip McCann and Luc Soete, *Place-Based Innovation for Sustainability* (Publications Office of the European Union, Luxembourg, 2020). DOI: 10.2760/250023.

53 UK MHRA (Medicines & Healthcare Products Regulatory Agency), "Guidance: assistive technology: definition and safe use." February 12, 2021. www.gov.uk/government/publications/assistive-technology-definition-and-safe-use/assistive-technology-definition-and-safe-use.

54 Amos Zehavi and Dan Breznitz, "Distribution sensitive innovation policies: conceptualization and empirical examples." *Research Policy* 46, no. 1 (2017): 327–336.

55 Jaideep Prabhu, "Frugal innovation: doing more with less for more." *Philosophical Transactions A* 375 (2017): 20160372, p. 1. http://dx.doi.org/10.1098/rsta.2016.0372

56 Gill Seyfang and Adrian Smith, "Grassroots innovations for sustainable development: towards a new research and policy agenda." *Environmental Politics* 16, no. 4 (2007): 584–603.

57 Aghion, Antonin, and Bunel, *The Power of Creative Destruction,* 176.

58 Jakob Edler and Jan Fagerberg, "Innovation policy: what, why and how." *Oxford Review of Economic Policy* 13, no. 1 (2017): 2–23; Johan Schot and W. Edward Steinmueller, "Three frames for innovation policy: R&D, systems of innovation and transformative change." *Research Policy* 47, no. 9 (2018): 1554–1567; Mariana Mazzucato, *Mission Economy: A Moonshot Guide to Changing Capitalism* (London: Penguin / Allen Lane, 2021).

59 Chesbrough coined the term "open innovation" in a 2003 *Harvard Business Review* piece. Henry W. Chesbrough, *Open Innovation: The New Imperative for Creating and Profiting from Technology* (Cambridge, MA: Harvard Business Review, 2003). See also Anne-Laure Mention and Marko Torkkeli, *Open Innovation: A Multifaceted Perspective* (Singapore: World Scientific, 2016).

60 Mirjam Burget, Emanuele Bardone, and Margus Pedaste, "Definitions and conceptual dimensions of responsible research and innovation: a literature review." *Science and Engineering Ethics* 23 (2017): 1–19.

61 For more on rural innovation, see Mahroum, Sami, Jane Atterton, Neil Ward, Allan M. Williams, Richard Naylor, Rob Hindle, and Frances Rowe, *Rural Innovation* (London: Nesta, December 1, 2007), 7.

62 Geoff Mulgan, Simon Tucker, Rushanara Ali, and Ben Sanders, "Social innovation: what it is, why it matters and how it can be accelerated." *Skoll Center for Entrepreneurship* (Oxford: University of Oxford, 2007), 8.

63 Jorge Saldivar, Cristhian Parra, Marcelo Alcaraz, Rebeca Arteta, and Luca Cernuzzi. "Civic technology for social innovation." *Computer Supported Cooperative Work (CSCW)* 28 (2018): 169–207.

64 For literature on systems innovation, see Barbara van Mierlo, Arni Janssen, Ferry Leenstra, and Ellen van Weeghel, "Encouraging system learning in two poultry subsectors. Agricultural systems" 115 (2013): 29–40; Barbara van Mierlo, Marlen Arkesteijn, and Cees Leeuwis, "Enhancing the reflexivity of system innovation projects with system analyses." *American Journal of Evaluation* 31, no. 2 (2010): 143–161; Charles Leadbetter and Jennie Winhall, "Building better systems: a green paper on systems innovation." Copenhagen: Rockwool Foundation, October 2020, p. 8.

65 Jamie Munger and Rudi Van Dael, *Putting People at the Heart of Policy Design: Using Human-Centered Design to Serve All* (Manila: Asian Development Bank, November 2020). www.adb.org/sites/default/files/publication/643866/people-policy-design-human-centered-design.pdf.

66 Arturo Escobar, *Designs for the Pluriverse* (Durham: Duke University, 2018); Ashish Kothari, Ariel Salleh, Arturo Escobar, Federico Demaria, and Alberto Acosta, *Pluriverse: A Post-Development Dictionary* (New York: Columbia University Press, 2019).

2 How

Innovation by and for problem-owners

This chapter explores innovation that aims to improve the material well-being of problem-owners, by strengthening their capabilities to drive or engage directly with ecosystems of opportunity that enhance the quality of life and work. In this part of the book, we compile cases and stories of innovation designed (by and for) various demographic groups, regions and sectors. We also highlight initiatives that seek to improve workplace processes and institutions towards greater productivity and higher incomes, or upgrade the infrastructure of people's daily lives in order to enable an improved experience (be that via access to employment, or through better health).

A key feature of this chapter's theme is its focus on economic, environmental and social contexts: interventions built up locally, with relevant and accessible interventions responsive to the kind of work around which local communities and economies are already anchored. It emphasizes innovation by the communities themselves, in which they are both the benefactors and beneficiaries of their own innovation, or innovating by, for, and of, rather than innovation being transferred or applied from elsewhere. We will explore different approaches and illustrations for making this come alive – from the emergent to more conventional – while also making the case for why including climate change and the environment is increasingly and crucially important. This "how" form of inclusive innovation is premised on the notion that society, especially the most economically vulnerable, and the ecological dimensions are inextricably intertwined. Innovation by and for the problem-owners then aims at meeting the local populations' needs, with environmental considerations at the heart of delivering on societal aims (Table 2.1).

As an example of this type of inclusive innovation, we look at the case of Peerathorn Seniwong (P'Thorn), who is a "saleng" (informal recycling collector) in the Prawet district situated on the outskirts of Bangkok. He didn't always live there: in 2001 local government officials told P'Thorn and his neighbors, who used to live under a bridge in the urban center, that they needed to relocate. He not only helped lead the negotiations but also took the initiative to ensure that his community would be able to support each other in the process.

DOI: 10.4324/9781003125877-2

Table 2.1 How: key concepts and sections

Key concepts	Design principles; grassroots innovation; HCD; social entrepreneurship; social innovation; systems innovation.
Sections	How can social capital boost inclusion?
	How can design principles encourage inclusion?
	How can grassroots innovation propel inclusive innovation?
	How can social innovation support inclusive innovation?
	How can systems innovation foster inclusive innovation?
	How can social and systems entrepreneurship drive inclusive innovation?
	Who is involved in this approach, and how?
	Strengths and shortcomings.

Today when you visit P'Thorn you can also see the co-op model he's been stewarding – the Zero Baht Shop (ZBS) – named in 2009 after years of experimenting with a bottom-up, community-driven approach to converting collected recyclables into cash for goods and services. The larger quantities of trash, organized and collated by the ZBS members, enable them to use collective power rather than a go-it-alone, competitive approach. What distinguishes ZBS is that the additional services they have generated to meet their own needs, and the money they receive from the recycling, goes to stock the shelves of their shop. Beyond the cashless Shop itself, where literally no "baht" (Thailand's currency) changes hands, only food and goods "purchased" with trash can be accessed. The ZBS model is innovative, as it offers alternative, nonmonetary "salaries" or "returns" that meet the needs of members and bring value through the exchange of community assets. There is an urban micro-farm to source fresh vegetables, and also sophisticated safety nets available to co-op members. The vision to meet community members' needs has grown to include stipends for education, subsidies for medical treatment, rice for the elderly, and even support for funeral fees. The only requirement to "opt-in" to the co-op is to bring one-baht worth of trash to ZBS on a daily basis, or 30 baht (just less than one $US1) worth monthly.[1] Explaining the aim of ZBS, P'Thorn said:

> We come to think about how to take care of community members. We want to put them on good welfare while they are still alive. We then launched a welfare scheme to provide relief for our community members by using waste as a link.

(P'Thorn[2])

For more on the story of the Zero Baht Shop, see Box 2.1.

Box 2.1 Zero Baht Shop: community co-ops and participatory innovation

By Chris Oestereich, Linear to Circular

Peerathorn Seniwong, P'Thorn to those who know him, lives in Prawet, a suburb on the outskirts of Bangkok, Thailand. P'Thorn works in the informal waste sector, as most people in his community do. While most people who perform such work do so in predefined roles, P'Thorn approaches it differently. In doing so, he improves his circumstances along with those of his community members.

Through his work, P'Thorn observed that informal waste collectors in his community faced a number of obstacles, including risks to their personal safety and unreliable incomes. One of the biggest challenges was that they lacked the ability to influence the system that provided their income. Having no real bargaining power, informal waste collectors have no other choice but to accept the daily rate they are given, which is typically low. Their only other option is to perform other work, if any can be found.

The system often leaves informal waste collectors unable to cover their subsistence and stagnant in their socioeconomic conditions. The cycle of poverty can be self-reinforcing.

Given his difficult circumstances, and the lack of alternatives, P'Thorn looked for ways to change the system. His first idea was to aggregate materials with his community members. Doing so would allow them to sell larger volumes at higher rates. If the daily rate for a kilogram of waste PET bottles was eight baht, a metric ton of the same material might get ten or more baht per kilogram. If they could deliver enough material to earn the higher rates, all who participated would increase the income they made for the same work.

Initially, the community was skeptical of P'Thorn's idea, so he launched a pilot program to test the opportunity. By directly showing how it could work, he was able to prove the case for his idea, while building trust with his community. In doing so, he fostered systemic change that has been replicated in other informal waste collector communities.

Over time, P'Thorn's informal project evolved into a waste collector co-op that developed additional programs to improve lives in his community. One of those is a convenience store where people trade recyclable goods for other useful items – the Zero Baht Shop. The Zero Baht initiative involved a two-step process: first, going to a location to redeem plastic and then, second, going shopping and streamlining the service. Together, the shop allows workers in the informal waste sector to have one space where they could efficiently bring their goods and shop.

Everything is purchased through a point system that is based on recyclable material collected.

At first, there was hesitation in reaction to the idea, but P'Thorn's pilot program was positively received amongst his community and many became convinced to join the co-op. Working together proved to be financially beneficial for the community, and as more people joined in, the revenue increased. In addition, another attractive feature that led to an influx of community members participating in the shop was its efficiency: it saved them a lot of time that was spent getting basic household goods from stores.

The high degree of collaboration, involvement, and incentives to earn higher rewards has resulted not only in more efficiency in the informal waste sector, but a strong community bond. The community has used some of their proceeds to build public infrastructure, such as a community garden, a health insurance program, and banking and funeral services. A self-sustained organic farm was also created in the process. The Zero Baht Shop in some ways has closed a gap by enabling the poorest communities in Bangkok to feel the positive impact of the recycling plant. Through the Zero Baht Shop economic stability and opportunities for future generations have been strengthened.

Building on the success of the Zero Baht Shop, P'Thorn is now taking his expertise elsewhere, sharing his process with other groups. P'Thorn has worked with the Thailand Institute of Packaging and Recycling Management for Sustainable Environment to create "sustainable community waste management solutions," spreading the tool of community power. He hopes to inspire other, and informal sector workers, to come together to develop solutions that benefit them and their communities, as the Zero-Baht shop has done for informal waste collectors in Bangkok. In the future, P'Thorn would like to see the model he created spread to university campuses as well.

How can social capital boost inclusion?

Social capital consists of one's relationships as well as experience and background.[3] Putnam defines social capital as "features of social organization such as networks, norms, and social trust that facilitate coordination and cooperation for mutual benefit."[4] This has implications for inclusion in innovation, as Klingler-Vidra and Liu assert, since "without personal connections, and without indications of the 'right' experiences and networks, underrepresented demographic groups may struggle to break into employment in innovative sectors."[5] Their study of inclusive innovation policies finds that policymakers are using social capital accumulation strategies to remedy such deficiencies by forging connections across members of innovation systems.

An example of an initiative boosting social capital for inclusion in the wider South Asian context is the Feminist Approaches to Labour Collectives, or FemLab.Co, founded in 2020. Its founding was motivated by the desire to explore how women are involved in the gig economy in India. See Box 2.2 on FemLab.Co for more.

Box 2.2 FemLab.Co: Bangladesh and India

When Payal Arora co-founded Feminist Approaches to Labor Collectives, or "FemLab.Co," in 2020, the desire to explore how women are involved in the gig economy in India and Bangladesh was fueled by the need to understand what needs to be done to enable female entrepreneurs to work considering the local cultural and systemic barriers they face. A seed-funded initiative by the International Development Research Centre (IDRC), FemLab.Co focuses on six specific labor spaces; construction, artisanal work, the garment sector, salon services, ride-hailing, and domestic work.

The organization additionally investigates the structural inhibitors to women's empowerment when attempting to incorporate the gig economy. Among the findings, a few stand out: the emergence of a safe space for women to share their views of the market while riding to work together, such as discussions surrounding how much other women make and how they work, which they also do on WhatsApp.

India's cultural and socioeconomic structure provides certain women, including those in higher castes, with fewer opportunities to work, namely due to the stigma surrounding women working as being a sign of financial trouble. Witnessing changes in the way women work in India and Bangladesh, the FemLab.Co initiative strives to provide women with the relevant tools and create knowledge that is needed for women's voices to be included in the discussions on the future of work. The initiatives work to include women in the discussion by first establishing who has access to digital media and therefore who gets to be heard. FemLab.Co is focused on the three following key points:

1. Building user and stakeholder insight through ethnographic engagement.
2. Making legal knowledge accessible by utilizing multimedia storytelling.
3. Guiding ethical design and deployment for the workers who are at the bottom of the supply chain.

FemLab.Co also explores the hindrances of getting paid and the gendered aspect of this kind of work while focusing on women's precarious position in the informal work market. Arora highlights women's exclusion, for example, "when union meetings are scheduled at inconvenient times for women" due to their domestic responsibilities, leaving them out of these formal solidarities.

FemLab.Co's initiative supports the collective agency of women workers who are at the bottom of supply chains by leveraging digital tools and bringing in more transparency. By recentering women workers in the design of platforms for work, FemLab.Co innovates with women who are socially and digitally organizing themselves and operating outside of conventional innovative clusters due to the widespread use of the internet. FemLab.Co nonetheless considers the local cultural norms and traditions that constitute barriers to women's access to innovative resources, including digital technology. In the same vein, their research has shown that women negotiate their way through to work online, obtaining "social permission" to take part in reselling, and navigating social relations with their male family members in order to access digital technology, such as mobile devices.

As illustrated by FemLab.Co, exclusion is more than a function of financial capital; inclusion and exclusion, in terms of innovation, is shaped by a combination of different types of capital – such as cultural, economic, human and social capital.[6] The propensity for exclusion on account of human and social capital is especially strong in the context of the knowledge economy, given the nature of higher, and often ICT-related, skills.[7]

Research on innovation has, at the margins, applied social capital theory to gain a better understanding of the formation and function of innovation systems. Such research employs social capital concepts particularly in theorizing the culture and competition elements of effective innovation systems. Akçomak and ter Weel, for instance, find that social capital is a lubricant for innovation systems, as "the financing of risky innovative projects requires that researchers and capital providers trust each other."[8]

The debate carries over into studies that explore whether social capital encourages or impedes activities such as high-growth entrepreneurship. In this capacity, Levitte explains that networks and positive values act as a support for would-be entrepreneurs, facilitating the establishment of trust that propels access to finance, service providers, and other resources.[9] There is also a downside to social capital, though, in that it can come with "conformity bias within tight groups, both regarding values and ideas, which may form a barrier" for heterogeneous participation.[10] The social capital of a particular place or environment may close off its existing inhabitants from new people and new ways of thinking, thereby acting as a barrier to innovation and entrepreneurship. As one of our advisors remarked, "innovation lives in the edges of the known"; if we don't go beyond those edges, then the potential for innovation is stunted. Homogeneity can fuel a negative form of social capital, driving conformity amongst the in-group and exclusion of those conceived of as being on the outside.

How can design principles encourage inclusion?

It is difficult to explore inclusive innovation, and how it is achieved, without touching on the philosophy of design.[11] According to Manzini, on the basis of design, we are all social innovators.[12] Yet, innovation is often associated with the model of Silicon Valley, anchored by dreams of disruption and the quest for "unicorns."[13] Yet these "designed" centers of innovation studies have generated significant inequity.[14] There have been efforts to try and recreate this Silicon Valley model in Southeast Asia. However, as Rex Lor, at the UNDP Accelerator Lab in the Philippines, explained in our Inclusive Innovation Stories and Learning Labs, the model is nonetheless only helpful to a limited extent, because the solutions to problems may induce more problems, or lead to unintended consequences. The notion, then, centers on envisaging locally-relevant models and processes.

With time, the "applied design" field – often referred to as a tool, mindset, or methodology for systems, service, or product design – has been used to catalyze innovation.[15] There are a number of design-meets-innovation process permutations, including "user-centered design," "participatory design," "design thinking," and HCD with the last notably having strong exportation from Silicon Valley. While the direction of the design process can be agnostic, its application (as most things in any social system) becomes mired in assumptions, bias, judgment, and values. To confront this limitation, HCD's evolving process has led designers to incorporate anthropology tools, such as ethnography, in order to better understand inclusion, equity, and accessibility.

What does design-driven inclusive innovation look like in practice? "The Hub of Innovation for Inclusion" in the Philippines gives us details, as found in Box 2.3.

HiFi, and others advancing a similar HCD approach, offer an alternative to technology-centric design paths. At the same time, we also ask: will a move towards socioecological considerations being placed on par with human considerations, known as *non-human-centric* design, help the advance of inclusive innovation? We can already see some emergent examples in the legal domain. For instance, in 2008 the Ecuadorian government inculcated "nature's legal rights" into their constitution; Bolivia followed a similar process three years later, and New Zealand has granted legal status to the Te Awa Tupua river, recognized in courts as an ancestor of the local Maori tribes.[16] In this regard, the question of who is design for – people as well as planet – carries weight.

Box 2.3 Hub of Innovation for Inclusion (HiFi)

By Francisco Moreno Jr, HiFi

A pioneer in the field, the Hub of Innovation for Inclusion (HiFi) in Manila, the Philippines, is an innovation office that welcomes new, progressive ideas from individuals who are focused on helping others and the planet through profit-generating and purpose-driven projects. Providing coaching and a space for ideas to be bounced around in search of innovative solutions to common problems, the HiFi works as a step-by-step process that invites individuals to share their ideas and projects, irrespective of the stage they have reached, in order to foster sustainable solutions to social problems. After witnessing dozens of fantastic innovative ideas go to waste after students' thesis were graded and subsequently left aside without actionable steps, the De La Salle College of Saint Benilde founded HiFi as an area for young entrepreneurs to continue sharing their ideas and get feedback.

In an interview with Adobo Magazine, founder and former-HiFi Director Abigail Mapua-Cabanilla shared the goal of creating an environment where young people could exchange their innovative ideas. More specifically, HiFi finds inclusion at the heart of its values, namely by showcasing the voices of those who are often last to be included, their goal being to include the "lost and the least among us," and therefore to investigate and solve problems that are complex, social, and environmental. HiFi ultimately serves as an incubator for tech, governance, and social innovation while also providing support for disaster mapping among other services.

Perhaps the most interesting aspect of the HiFi is its innovation-provoking process. The four-step journey begins on the ground floor of the building. The "Empathy Hall," as it is called, is the initial view when one enters the building. The vicinity is open to all who would like to join discussions or programs taking place. Concerns, problems, and ideas are shared with the community in order to foster innovation and further discussions.

The second stage of the process is located on the second floor, called the bright space. There's a pantry at the back, private rooms, and desks open to anyone's disposal. The second floor is where innovators work on solving problems that have been brought up on the ground floor, from being environmentally-driven to being focused on social equality.

The third floor, and third stage, is where team activities take place. Called the "Maker Space," workshops take place in this area. 3-D printers are available and prototypes can be created. The tools needed to innovate are all there, ready to be used by whoever is in need today.

The space is additionally easily changed into one that accommodates training and workshops based on the skills needed to be developed.

Finally, the fourth floor is, perhaps metaphorically, on the roof where the air is fresh and the ideas flow freely. This section is called the "Evergreen" area, and is where pitches take place. The final stages occur here, and then a celebration entails when the product or service can be launched. There are inspirational statements plastered over the walls, and an environment of anticipation and excitement fills the room. And just like this, an idea has made it past the four steps – the four floors – of product creation.

Rather than focusing on tech solutions to simple problems, the HiFi focuses on solving complex problems that follow a HCD. Instead of attempting to include everyone, the innovators' voices that are included are those that are usually marginalized or forgotten. Not only are the projects themselves inclusive of marginalized communities, but the innovators too are young people who may struggle to have access to entrepreneurial ecosystems. Expanding on this, Mapua-Cabanilla explained that putting a bridge between different actors in various sectors is a main goal behind the HiFi. Industry leaders, academia members, or government representatives are used to working within their own organizations. HiFi, on the contrary, wants to allow students to make meaningful connections while also fostering more collaboration between various kinds of organizations, including NGOs, governments, the private sector, and other sectors. Moreover, the organization supports the inclusion of young entrepreneurs by building strategic partnerships with stakeholders as well as ecosystem developers. Finally, they partner up with organizations involved in governance, including the government and banks.

It means design processes for inclusive innovation that target sustainable and regenerative ecosystem possibilities.[17]

How can grassroots innovation propel inclusive innovation?

Grassroots innovation can be described in various ways – as a process and in terms of its outcome. It involves a bottom-up approach, generating from civil society rather than government or (big) business, often driving towards broader social change and addressing challenges in the local context.[18] It is understood as something that can happen at three levels – individual, group, and societal.[19] In addition to the multiple levels, as noted in the UNESCAP *Policies and Strategies to Promote Grassroots Innovation* report, grassroots innovations can emerge in different ways: spontaneously (to meet a need in a low-resource environment), induced (when an external actor incentivizes), and through co-creation (often when an external actor facilitates an innovation process).[20]

The origin story of grassroots innovation is not a new one. In India, for example, since the 1980s, through the Honey Bee Network, thousands of volunteers have documented more than one million ideas, innovations, and traditional knowledge practices. To find them, the volunteers take exploration journeys, or "Shodh Yatras" in Hindi, where volunteers visit local communities searching for grassroots innovations. If a grassroots innovation is considered to be an indicator of an unmet need, then by systematically identifying and helping diffuse grassroots innovations, the "net effect" can be significant if explored at scale.[21] Through its decades of work, the Honey Bee Network has helped draw attention to grassroots innovation in Southeast Asia.[22] As understood by the Honey Bee Network, grassroots innovation is considered a form of inclusive innovation that enables extremely affordable, niche-adapted solutions to local problems, often unaided by the public sector or outsiders.[23]

Typically, grassroots innovators develop their ideas when existing solutions are inefficient, unaffordable, or inaccessible. In some ways whether or not a grassroots innovation will be adopted depends on context – preexisting social capital networks, location, and timing.[24] Examples of mainstream grassroots innovation are happening in the Philippines where the Grassroots Innovation for Inclusive Development (GRIND) of the Department of Science & Technology (DOST) Region XI, in collaboration with the UNDP Philippines, has formally launched a systematic "Solutions Mapping" initiative: "*SalikLakbay*. A combination of the words 'Saliksik' (to explore or research) and 'Lakbay' (to journey or go on an adventure), it aims to equip participants with the background knowledge, skills, and practical experience needed in order to conduct solutions mapping in grassroots communities."[25] The overarching objective is to build the grassroots to government infrastructure, one that can enable better diffusion and incubation.

How can social innovation support inclusive innovation?

Social innovation is a type of innovation that emphasizes processes and how resources are organized to generate a positive impact in society. Mulgan and co-authors, for instance, emphasize social innovation as being characterized as: (1) usually new combinations or hybrids of existing elements, (2) operating across organizational, sectoral, or disciplinary boundaries, and (3) fostering new social relationships between previously separate individuals and groups that fuel the possibility of further innovation.[26] In a similar way, Morris-Suzuki and Soh identify core elements as: (1) meeting a social need, (2) effectiveness, (3) novelty, (4) moving from ideas to implementation, and (5) enhancing society's capacity to act.[27] Others bring in the moral imperative by defining social innovation as "a novel solution to a social problem that is more effective, efficient, sustainable, or *just* than present solutions."[28] Given the importance of collaboration across individuals and groups, other definitions emphasize the social *management* of innovation, where the process of management itself is innovative, stressing the importance of how people and resources are organized.

Social innovation may be "characterized by conceptual ambiguity and a diversity of definitions."[29] In fact, investigations attempting to uncover convergence have found "76 different definitions" of social innovation.[30] While some remark that the general lack of clarity impedes the sophistication of the field in terms of advancing useful learning to be leveraged at scale,[31] others argue that embracing the diversity of interpretations and how it *differs* from business and technological innovation proves more helpful.[32] To this end, Ziegler suggests framing social innovation as a "collaborative" concept so that actors in the ecosystem can carve out space to work more intentionally.[33] Similarly, the Australian Centre for Social Innovation suggests collective action-oriented intelligence and a road map that points towards developing "Social R&D" that is inclusive, informs decision-making, and accelerates the sharing of ideas. In practice it means ensuring that communities and individuals, including those at the margins, are directly engaged in agenda-setting, decision-making, and power structures at multiple levels.[34] The democratization of who is driving innovation is also aligned with "citizen science" movements, which is characterized by "active public involvement in scientific research" that is growing "bigger, more ambitious, and more networked."[35]

Seen through the perspectives outlined above, we consider social innovation in terms of networking and collaboration that transcends the "innovator as hero" narratives. Instead of individuals, inclusive innovations tend to come from multiple stakeholders. They can also stem from social movements and the wider public consciousness that they bring.[36]

How can systems innovation foster inclusive innovation?

There are overlapping threads that emerge when attempting to define "systems innovation." We explore this concept from the lens of "systemic innovation," which is defined as an "interconnected set of innovations, where each influences the other, with innovation both in the parts of the system and in the ways in which they interconnect."[37] Systems are complex and require intervention at a foundational level.

A key concern is who is included in the system. Systems innovation interventions typically engage across three levels: the macro, meso, and micro.[38] One may ask how any set of actors operate in this complex change model? In many ways it's about understanding both the nature of the complex challenges and how systems form and who is initiating and leading change. As Odin Mühlenbein notes, systems innovation does not need to drive full systems overhauls; the aims and actions can be incremental so long as they are aimed at the system.[39]

Intervening in and changing systems is enhanced by being able to see challenges and opportunities in new ways. Leadbetter and Winhall explain that systems innovation can be considered twofold: *responding* or *realizing* an opportunity connected to a complex problem.[40] For an applied example we can look to the Climate- Knowledge and Innovation Community (KIC), Europe's largest public-private innovation partnership focused on climate innovation, as it defines systems innovation "as integrated and coordinated interventions in economic, political, technological and social systems and along whole value chains." This approach "seeks to engage and interact with all levers of change" across hard (policy, regulatory frameworks, financing models) and soft (social norms, behaviors, identities, and narratives) domains.[41]

Said simply, systems are central to inclusive innovation, for there is no inclusion without there being something to be included into. In Southeast Asia, we can learn about system-oriented inclusive innovation from the experience of Pulse Lab Jakarta. As Petrarca Karetji, its head of office, points out, the organization is shifting in terms of reframing its systems approach. In reflecting upon its evolution, it has come to better understand the nature of its position and the evolving problems.[42] In particular, it is calling for stronger standards to support collaboration and avoid the inefficiency that can come from competition. One tack that it is taking is to initiate processes such as "sensemaking" that allows it to surface internal insights.

Another example of a systems approach to inclusive innovation is WeSolve, an incubator and accelerator in the Philippines that works to bring social change in different sectors through the power of collective action. Co-founded by management and development consultants Rapa and Jaime Lopa, a volunteer and advocate duo, the team employs mainly young individuals. The organization has been working with civil society, nongovernmental organizations (NGOs), communities, governments, and citizens all over the Philippines to address social issues.[43]

As an illustration of how it operates, WeSolve supports the Citizens' Budget Tracker, a community effort to hold power to account by tracking the national budget. Through budget tracking, research, and advocacy, the Citizens' Budget Tracker helps civil society coalitions engage in the budget cycle; with better data on public budget use, citizens will be better able to challenge, and engage with, government. Another example comes from WeSolve's work on building a future-proof circular food system for Metro Manila, where it is mapping the food system and co-designing market-based solutions to the hunger and undernutrition problem. By harnessing emerging models and partnerships to close gaps in the food system, the project aims to improve access to nutritious food for urban and rural poor households. Through its numerous projects, WeSolve operates according to the mantra of "making together work" through its collaboration with a diverse range of communities and marginalized groups.

In thinking about systems innovation, it is also helpful to consider a sociotechnical framework. As underscored by Geels and co-authors, "socio-technical transitions gain momentum when multiple innovations are linked together, improving the functionality of each and acting in combination to reconfigure systems."[44] With this in mind, we share "inclusive approaches" observable in practice across the innovation landscape, while also noting transformation frameworks that invite us to consider just where and how these approaches are positioned.[45]

We also consider the notion of *transformational change*, which has roots in organizational theory for over three decades, and its application to a socioecological context is increasingly acknowledged. Waddock and Wadell contend that there are two approaches converging.[46] One comes from the environmental tradition and centers around mitigation, adaptation, and transformation; the other comes from sociology and management and emphasizes learning loops.[47] However, others have argued that thinking in terms of incremental and transformative change is not necessarily a useful construct.[48] Navigating change across the inclusive innovation spectrum, they assert, is contextual, and categories such broad categories are too widely cast.

As our advisor Kelly Ann McKercher asserts, all the different paths available are not necessarily visible. In Box 2.4, she shares her thoughts on the downside of categories and the pursuit of quick wins; she makes the case for thinking in terms of "choose your own adventure," in order to drive transformative change.

Box 2.4 Choosing your adventure

By Kelly Ann McKercher, Beyond Sticky Notes

When I was younger, I loved "choose your adventure" books. I'd explore each pathway to avoid a dead-end and get the best outcome. Unfortunately, in attempting inclusive innovation, the alternative paths aren't visible enough, and we may not get to choose.

Despite the ongoing disruption of COVID-19, innovation approaches derived by and for private businesses continue to dominate. Such methods have normalized decision-making for communities (often without meaningful community partnership) and often reinforce exclusion through innovators reproducing harms such as ableism, heteronormativity, the gender binary, and white supremacy. Beyond this world of listicles that promises quick wins (e.g. seven ways to radically transform your organization) is a movement of organizers and co-designers shaping different worlds. Here are two alternatives:

1. Embrace co-planning, co-design, co-delivery and co-evaluation to reduce gaps between what decision-makers think people need and what people actually need.

2. Adapt or discard mainstream innovation methods (such as design sprints or writing ideas on sticky notes) to broaden who can discover and design. Learn with or be led by artists, disabled communities, queer communities, and First Nations.

So, how can we make alternatives visible so that we can choose different futures?

How can social and systems entrepreneurship drive inclusive innovation?

Seminal definitions, like that of Peredo and McLean, assert that there are five key attributes that define social entrepreneurship.[49] They say that it is exercised when a person or group (1) aim(s) to create social value, either exclusively or at least in some prominent way, (2) show(s) a capacity to recognize and take advantage of opportunities to create that value, (3) employ(s) innovation, ranging from outright invention to adapting someone else's novelty, in creating and/or distributing social value, (4) is/are willing to accept an above-average degree of risk in creating and disseminating social value, and (5) is/are unusually resourceful in being relatively undaunted by scarce assets in pursuing their social venture.

For systems entrepreneurs (increasingly called "systempreneurs"), Schaile et al. offer a definition.[50] First, the existence of high uncertainty. Second and third, respectively, the potential for a system-changing entrepreneurial solution and co-creation, and fourth, and finally, the fact that systems entrepreneurs are aware of, and oriented towards, their embedding in a broader system. There are multiple places for systems entrepreneurs to intervene in innovation systems, at different levels of change and through a range of possible entrepreneurial and (non)commercial actions.

Like the other concepts discussed, the fields of social entrepreneurship and systems entrepreneurship are full of divergent opinions and unsettled agreement.[51] What we observe is a field in evolution – where the intention to collaborate more effectively occurs as the "transformative potential of entrepreneurship does not simply arise from the genius of apt individuals or organizations (so-called 'heropreneurs')."[52] This goes beyond providing discrete solutions, and instead strives for changes to the architecture of a system.[53] It considers that both innovation and entrepreneurship are nested and dependent on institutions, including culture and social relations, as power dynamics again come into play.[54] Box 2.7, at the end of this chapter, offers Julien Leyre's story of inclusive innovation that pushes past the idea of the heropreneur, and makes us think about the importance of both failure and inclusion in a system of innovation.

There are nuanced distinctions between social entrepreneurs and systems entrepreneurs. Social entrepreneurs work often in precarious, underresourced settings, to address and mitigate immediate, bounded social issues. Social entrepreneurs may also strengthen wider systems, but that is not necessarily their intent. Their aims tend to be more focused. In contrast, systems, entrepreneurs aim to shift broader systems, thereby the intent is often what distinguishes one from the other. Our advisor, Odin Mühlenbein, shares his thoughts on systems social entrepreneurs, which brings the two concepts together, based on his work at Ashoka, as detailed in Box 2.5.

As pointed out by Knox and Tan, there needs to be a shift whereby social entrepreneurs adopt a system change approach, one "in which the problem accurately reflects the experience and input of the problem-owners, and indeed includes them in the development of solutions."[55] In short, contributors,

---

Box 2.5 Systems social entrepreneurs

By Odin Mühlenbein, Ashoka

Systems social entrepreneurs focus on the root causes of social problems. Instead of treating symptoms, they change policies, practices, industry standards, power dynamics, and social norms. They don't just help a few thousand students to become better in Maths; they change the education system so that in the whole country produces fewer students who are struggling. They don't just sell fair trade clothes; they change industry standards to lower the ecological footprint of entire value chains. In the words of Thomas Sattelberger, a Member of Parliament in Germany, "Social innovators are transformational guides for societal issues."

Ashoka is the world's largest network of systems social entrepreneurs. Together with Catalyst 2030, Echoing Green, Schwab, Skoll, and McKinsey, we recently published the report "New Allies: how governments can unlock the potential of social entrepreneurs for the common good." Our recommendations are based on the best practices from five continents. If you want social entrepreneurs to make your societies more inclusive and sustainable, it's clear what you need to do:

1. Co-create and share data!
2. Train civil servants and systems social entrepreneurs!
3. Invest in social innovations just like you do in technological innovations!
4. Promote collaboration among the public, private, and social sectors!
5. Institutionalize successful social innovations via government programs and policies!

such as social enterprises, must be conceived of as part of a broader system, and that system needs to enable their work from multiple dimensions. Papi-Thornton argues that "when those who know little about a complex social or environmental challenge are asked to propose solutions, they often barely scratch the surface of the issue."[56] To counter this, she has been working to transform the heropreneurship tendency towards one where entrepreneurs own their problem, not the solution. To contend that one is able to offer *the* solution is in many ways a fallacy in the context of complex challenges.

Who is involved in this approach, and how?

Academia has a significant role to play when it comes to advancing the inclusive innovation ecosystem from a practical lens, in addition to conducting research on the subject. For example, the South East Asia Social Innovation Network (SEASIN) was established in 2016 to support and promote social innovation as an avenue for generating inclusive growth and equity. Although the network is cross-sector, the majority of partners are academic institutions that drive scale with thousands of students participating.[57] Their model is designed for reach through Social Innovation Support Units that are embedded at 11 university campuses across 7 countries. The idea is to ensure that there is a dedicated physical space (i.e. maker space, incubators) where students, faculty, and the ecosystem at large can collaborate on social innovation-oriented projects.

Another example is the Universities and Councils Network on Innovation for Inclusive Development in Southeast Asia[58] (UNIID-SEA), based at the Ateneo School of Government under the Ateneo de Manila University and the National Research Council of the Philippines. The four main goals of the latter project are to foster (1) field-building, (2) paradigm shifts in higher education and research, (3) building a community of excellence, and (4) policy contribution at the national and ASEAN levels. In both examples we see an externally-funded (the EU, and Canada's IDRC, respectively) networked platform approach to accelerating the ecosystem.

Central to the role of academia is changing the narrative about who is an innovator, what "counts" as innovation (e.g. not only Silicon Valley-styled heropreneurs), and how innovation happens. On the basis of his experience as both an academic and practitioner working throughout Latin America, Omar Crespo Cardona shares his thoughts about how academics can deliver on this aim as presented in Box 2.6.

Civil society, as problem-owners and problem-solvers, are at the center of inclusive innovation. As mentioned earlier, social R&D could be one channel for engaging multiple actors, especially from civil society. As pointed out by the Asia Foundation's exploration into the effects of the COVID-19 pandemic, there is no one "best practice" to emulate, rather for each setting to strive to pursue a highly contextual response.[59] Other examples include Catalyst 2030, which has an active network across Southeast Asia, and is composed of

---

Box 2.6 Changing how innovation is taught

By Omar Crespo Cardona, Link4

Within innovation for development, we are seeing a trend that celebrates disruptive technologies that appear to be overnight successes and drastically transforming realities. And while they may happen, they are not the norm.

Having a foot in academia and mainly being a practitioner, I feel a responsibility to contribute to shift the innovation paradigm in development. We must teach that innovation is less about inventing and more about enabling; not about the heroic, glorious, and individual endeavor of saving communities, but instead about collaborating with them. Innovation needs to be inclusive and participatory. And this requires significant preparation and background work that is often overlooked and unrecognized. It is key to make sure the right actors are participating, and that the right conditions and capacities exist to allow the participation to be effective and for everyone involved to feel heard and comfortable sharing their experiences, opinions, and ideas.

A common ground must be built and the efforts to join it need to be bidirectional. Participatory design skills and mindsets are essential elements for inclusive innovation. These types of analytical and iterative thinking are not native to humans, they need to be learned. At the same time, local and ancestral wisdom needs to be seen, heard, understood, and honored. It is in the intersection where these elements coexist, that I believe, the true and less celebrated potential of innovation lies – to build resilience, empowerment, leadership, self-reliance, and to strengthen the local innovation ecosystem in a sustainable and long-lasting way.

"innovators from all sectors who share the common goal of creating innovative, people-centric approaches to attain the SDGs by 2030."[60]

Funders and investors have an important role to play when it comes to incentivizing inclusive innovation with social and environmental targets. Investors, striving to deliver on their investment mandates, set the direction for inclusion and social impact for entrepreneurs for years to come, however their relatively short-term aims (e.g. to exit within the 10-year lifespan of their limited partnership fund) can run counter to that potential.[61] Despite the potential for inclusive finance, there remains a multitrillion investment gap to meet the ambitions of the SDGs. This space is particularly crucial to watch as the effects of the pandemic have disrupted and altered the conventional status quo in many places. The common denominators that hold the inclusive finance approach together include "(1) intent, (2) understanding evolutionary possibilities, (3) leveraging system dynamics, (4) blending for synergistic effects, and (5) evaluation as transformational return on investment."[62] Take, for example, the case of Vietnam, where the government, UNDP, the Embassy of Finland in Vietnam, and Climate-KIC are exploring the financing of a circular economy, one that requires a "transformation capital" logic model to usher the social, technological, and economic rewiring.[63]

However, the distinction is made between progressive capital (adjustments to the system) and transformation capital (transformation to the system) and how goals, power dynamics, intent, action strategy, and logic, are distinct.[64] We can observe the call in the *C40 Mayors' Agenda for a Green and Just Recovery*, committing to:

> Ensure stimulus investment and recovery funds create more just and inclusive societies and communities and directly address long-standing inequalities and ongoing discrimination based on race.[65]

For on-the-ground examples, we can look to the IIX's Women's Livelihood Bond 2 – a blended finance approach integrating a gender lens into a stock-exchange-listed impact fund through the Zero Gap Fund.[66] In 2020, just as the pandemic was unfolding, Cambodia's Amru Rice (a locally owned rice exporter) was able to leverage investment from this structure, which helped ensure supply chain resiliency. The Zero Gap Fund offers a powerful example of an innovative means of financing, one which helps incentivize investment towards environmental and social problems.

Governments and international organizations play a role in advancing inclusive innovation. Interesting approaches include Coalitions for Change,[67] a program that strives to equip cross-sector local leaders with the skills and guidance needed to champion policy inclusive reforms. This initiative is carried out in the Philippines (2018–2022) through a partnership between the government, the Australian Department of Foreign Affairs and Trade, and the Asia Foundation. It is designed to be adaptive and has pivoted its approach throughout the pandemic, away from conventional development programming. In terms of accelerating innovation from the wider society, in Thailand the National Higher Education Science Research and Innovation Policy Council (NXPO) – a public agency affiliated to the Ministry of Higher Education, Science, Research and Innovation – has created channels such as the Thailand Innovation Policy Accelerator as well as sandboxes and systems research focusing on the future of education, the circular economy, and food systems.[68]

Public policymakers can also play a role in mitigating the potentially harmful impacts of new technologies and services. Scenario planning and other foresight methodologies have been used by governments to this end, as well as the use of "anticipatory regulation" tools and processes.[69] For example, the Energy Market Authority of Singapore has created a sandbox for energy innovations to assess the impact of new products and services before deciding on the appropriate way to regulate them. This design approach could be used even more explicitly to anticipate and mitigate ways in which innovations may be exclusive as well as inclusive.

Other examples from the region include the Royal Government of Cambodia's Ministry of Civil Service where they have, with technical support from UNDP Cambodia, been working towards (1) creating a risk space for inclusive innovation, (2) empowering civil servants with continuous innovation capacity, and (3) transforming citizen-centric public services through HCD and digitization. As pointed out by the UNDP team in Cambodia in their reflection, a word of caution:

> We often see that bureaucracies tend to explore only a small, fairly predictable subset of all possible solutions to a given problem, usually emanating from the top, central level of policy making. The solutions that are then chosen and implemented are in many cases the obvious but not necessarily most effective ones ... [and we need] to move beyond just methods and focus at the systemic level on building a mindset that allows us to tackle complex issues by taking an unconventional and experimental approach.[70]

Finally, the Philippines' Poverty Reduction through Social Entrepreneurship (PRESENT) Bill aims to empower social enterprises – with over 30,000 registered in the Philippines alone – to help them deliver on their potential to respond to the societal challenges faced by vulnerable populations.[71] In her discussion of the Bill and accompanying program in an April 2021 UNDP webinar on Building Back Better in the Philippines, Dr. Lisa Dacanay emphasized the need for the approach to be inclusive, in terms of having a variety of stakeholders at the table, with problem-owners at the center of efforts.[72]

Grassroots innovators will continue to grow the field of inclusive innovation by designing and implementing solutions that meet (their own) immediate needs. The critical opportunity for scale sits with the diffusion of ideas, and public policy can provide institutional and financial support to enable this.[73] The work of policies to enable grassroots innovators will be set up for wider adoption if there is support to (1) discover and promote grassroots innovations, (2) recognize and protect them, (3) incubate and commercialize these innovations, (4) socially or commercially diffuse grassroots innovations and knowledge, and (5) develop linkages among different actors of a grassroots innovation ecosystem.[74]

Intermediary organizations (accelerators / incubators) have space to drive inclusive innovation forward. A 2021 report by the Global Accelerator Learning Initiative (GALI), a collaboration between the Aspen Network of Development Entrepreneurs (ANDE) and Emory University, led an exploration into how acceleration and incubation services can support small and growing businesses.[75] In Southeast Asia, the Impact Hub and Frontier Incubators have localized processes and developed guides to support greater inclusion and diversity.[76] A crucial orientation is that intermediary organizations should strive to convene the collective in order to optimize collaboration while still enabling individuals, communities, and organizations to retain autonomy.[77]

Large firms can leverage their scale to shift the innovation landscape towards inclusion. Arguably this convention is not new – there have been many firms that have tried to incorporate "people and planet" into the core aims of their product and processes, to have a triple bottom line (TBL).[78] How inclusive they are can vary, yet the field is evolving and includes the growing roles of environmental, social, and governance (ESG) criteria that is measurable and are increasingly used by investors. Also, corporate social responsibility (CSR) is another framework for channeling market-based goodwill; this is a concept developed by Archie Carroll in 1979, referring to "a company's various voluntary initiatives towards its different stakeholders such as customers, suppliers, regulators, employees, investors, and communities."[79]

A variety of related vocabulary has developed over time, with similar notions of the social purpose of business activities. Notably, the idea of pursuing "profit with purpose"[80] and delivering "shared value"[81] speaks to the pursuit of both financial returns (profit) and business that has a positive impact on society.[82] Another example is BoP models, as mentioned in the opening chapter,[83] where both consumers and producers actively participate in driving innovation and growth. The incentives of BoP-serving firms are often reacting to perceived social injustice in dominant innovation paradigms. In the context of Southeast Asia, the number of inclusion-oriented businesses is still. Analysts have attributed this to systemic challenges, such as lower levels of education, inconsistent infrastructure, and inflexible regulatory environments.[84]

Startups and SMEs are the backbone of the ASEAN economic region, as they are in most places around the world. One advantage for SMEs innovating is their agility in operationalizing efforts, as decision-making can happen quickly since most are owner-managed. However, SMEs often lack the financial and technical know-how to conduct R&D, so they can operate at a lower, or second-speed, to that of large, multinational firms in terms of their innovation capacity.

Consistent with this chapter's focus on the role of systems and the collective, often it is the expertise of multiple actors working together, and closely with civil society and local communities, that leads to success. For example, the Pasar Sejahtera – or "prosperous market" – program mentioned earlier, which aims to increase the competitiveness of traditional markets, or pasar, to contend with the growth of modern supermarkets. Improvements to pasar as physical spaces encourage more local people to choose to shop there rather than in modern supermarkets, which are less tied into the local economy and community. They have leveraged the financial expertise of Yayasan Danamon Peduli, a nonprofit foundation, along with input from the Indonesian Ministry of Health and local government. Another approach comes from B Corp Asia, which announced a Southeast Asia Hub in 2021, and is working to certify 100 more businesses across the region by 2025; at the time of writing there are less than 20 currently on the roster in Singapore, Malaysia, and Indonesia.[85]

Strengths and shortcomings

A key strength of many of the "how" approaches is the emphasis on community embeddedness: most initiatives in this area make a great effort to work closely with local communities in creating solutions that are responsive to their needs. This type of activity therefore has the potential for lasting effects on its problem-owner communities, particularly when programs are oriented towards institutional and ecosystem change along with technology transfer, as in the case of Pasar Sejahtera, so that problem-owners are also crucial problem-solvers.

The involvement of multiple stakeholders (government, NGOs, charitable foundations, social enterprises) can be a great strength to an initiative, allowing a range of expertise, capabilities, and financing to drive the development and implementation of successful initiatives. Several interviewees noted the importance of public support for projects initiated from outside government, or local government support for projects initiated centrally. However, multi-stakeholder involvement can be a shortcoming if there is variable understanding between these stakeholders over goals and processes. For example, the World Bank initiated the VIIP in 2013, in partnership with two government bodies: the Ministry of Planning and Investment (MPI) and the National Foundation for Science and Technology Development (NAFOSTED).[86] The VIIP, in partnership with Vietnam's MPI, was focused on the intentionality of inclusive innovation. Its objective was as follows:

> To adopt, upgrade and develop inclusive innovations for the benefit of the Base of Pyramid population (BoP), by: (i) strengthening the recipient's capacity to undertake Inclusive Innovation, including financing development, adaptation, adoption, scale-up and commercialization of Inclusive Technologies; and (ii) improving Research and Development Institutions' (RDIs) and small and medium enterprises' (SMEs) technological and innovation capabilities.[87]

The focus on inclusive innovation was the result of an appraisal identifying that "Vietnam was experiencing rapid and consistent economic growth accompanied by overall poverty reduction, yet inequities were increasing."[88]

However, the VIIP's impact was limited due to challenges associated with operationalizing inclusive innovation in practice. Specifically, the different teams struggled to agree and operationalize the criteria by which applicants were measured, which inhibited the distribution of project funds.[89] This underscores the tension. There is a clear opportunity for governments and international organizations to benefit from working closely with inclusive innovators, given their efforts to find solutions to systemic or complex social

Box 2.7 On failure and inclusion in the innovation narrative

By Julien Leyre

'No globe, no fun' used to be the motto when I worked at the Global Challenges Foundation. No matter what you care about, whether it's LGBTIQ rights, women-run cooperatives, or indigenous arts, you need a planet for it. So, we gathered a team of do-gooders to try and reduce global catastrophic risk. What's more inclusive, after all, than preserving the basic conditions for human life on the planet? To get there, we organized a global prize competition, hoping to catch a few valuable ideas.

This was not my first gig. In 2005, I put together a queer anthology for teenagers. I was 27 then, looking for a way to bond with my 12-year-old half-brother: "Do you have a book with gay characters?" "Oh yes," said the person at the bookstore. She grabs a book, enthusiastic. "It's about this little boy who comes to terms with the death of his brother. He's diagnosed with HIV, and kills himself." I've never been one to complain and do nothing. So, we gathered a team of do-gooders, and put together Regardez Moi dans le Yeux, the first anthology of positive gay teenage stories to come out in Paris. Except, it was a small publishing house, version control got loose, one angry writer brought in the lawyers, and the book was taken off the shelves.

This was my first failure at inclusive innovation. In the 20th century, I was mainstream and lonely: straight white guy from a good school and a well-off family. In the new Millennium, I found belonging by becoming a minority. I came out, took over the LGBTIQ club in my college, and found my crew. But I wanted more than a bubble: I wanted a common world. So, it was posters and conversations – also, frankly, the best parties – and a book project. This only made failure more bitter. I later published another novel with that same publisher, but I did it alone. The book-team fell apart when Regardez Moi dans le Yeux went to pulp.

I can trace back the dream of building a common world to my early childhood. I grew up as the son of a Mediterranean father who settled in the European capital, and a wild mother of Italian background. The European dream was more than a matter of civic pride: historical maps, architecture, and accents reminded me that France had been an imperial overlord to the lands where I grew up, and my family lived. But we were all Europeans. Building supranational belonging could resolve tensions in my own identity, and bring together the people I loved.

This aim to drive inclusion became a lifelong mission. In 2006, Hospitality Club – the Euro version of Couchsurfing – brought an Australian into my life. I didn't freak out, or not too much: why not move across the globe? I could carry the European dream to the southern hemisphere. When I first visited Melbourne, I saw it as the cultural capital of a globalized world, where the traditions of Europe and Asia, colonial and indigenous histories, could come together. I moved in 2008, after a three-month overland trip from Paris to Singapore, and picked up Chinese as part of my self-styled, becoming-Australian project. Then in 2010, there was a middle-of-the-night vision, and I founded a charity: the Marco Polo Project, a collaborative translation platform bringing the voices of Chinese Intellectuals to Western readers – a first step towards global cultural integration. This project was about Melbourne as a place of radical inclusion, but it was also about the flourish of digital commons, back when Facebook was about friends, and Google about knowledge.

It was a crazy dream, yet I seemed to be pulling it off. I gathered volunteers, developers, authors, translators, and a touch of funding, or at least freebies – and not all of it purely through madness and French charm. Sure, the thing was completely not sustainable, but I had faith funding would come. The vision was good, it was on trend, it served a purpose. Meanwhile, I could hack the system. Downside, it meant I had to continue my old habit of wearing multiple hats. First, I was a founder and a government worker, then a founder and a freelance language teacher, then a founder and a startup incubator COO. Those were opportunistic identities. One stuck though: starting 2015, I was a founder and a PhD student on scholarship. The Marco Polo Project was nerdy, China was hot, tech was the future of education. So, I started research on the digital ecosystem of Chinese language learning, as a distributed public good in the making. I could give academic gravitas to my dream of global connection, and if I played my cards well, I could get a university to carry the vision forward.

It was a clear enough storyline, until I got a message from an old friend. Corin and I had met at the crossroads of queer activism and EU solidarity, organizing gay pride in Ljubljana, circa 2003. In February 2016, the Global Challenges Foundation was looking for an atypical profile to serve as Chief Editor. "Would you like to help us avoid the end of the world?" I'm not one to refuse joining the Avengers. As long as I didn't have to move to Sweden, I was in ... subzero temperatures don't really work for me.

It was a tough gig. It started with a vertical learning curve, then came emotional overload. That black box with ecosystem collapse and nuclear winter and super-volcanoes: I had to stare inside when I coordinated the world's first "concise introduction to global catastrophic risk" in 2017. But I was good at the job, it paid well, and there was a recognizable title. Now, I was a founder, PhD student, and chief editor, doing inclusive innovation in my own way: intercultural dialogue, EdTech as a global public good, and global governance innovation.

Cracks were already showing though. It's December 2016, and I'm walking down the aisle in the ballroom of the Victorian Governor's mansion. Gold on the walls, throne on the stage. It's Multicultural Awards day, and I'm runner-up for the top prize. As I walk to my seat on the front row, joyful thoughts echo in my head. I'm part of it now! I shake hands with the man seated next to me, handsome Mister First Prize. "I work with Afghan refugees in Dandenong," he shares, "I help them settle in Australia. What about you? What community are you from?" I blabber. "Well, I'm French, but I work with Chinese communities. And international students. We do collaborative translation events, in Melbourne, and around the world. I'm also doing a PhD on Chinese language learning. Oh, and I work on global catastrophic risk with a Swedish NGO." Eyes glazed, awkward smile, silence. No wonder I was a runner-up: outliers never win first prize.

The cracks widened. After the Foundation ran its prize competition in 2018, the team fell apart. Corin moved on to focus on governance innovation – a book, talks, and derived products followed. And I followed. I've always trusted people over organizations. But it was back to shapeless job descriptions and hacking the system. Meanwhile, my PhD findings were depressing. I was hoping to see clear signs of a digital ecosystem emerging. What I found instead was more like a handful of Quixotic dudes (it was all dudes) holding onto small startups against the odds, hacking the system to keep afloat. Meanwhile, the Marco Polo Project pivoted to local engagement under a new CEO. Three paths diverged in the woods, and I wasn't sure which one would make all the difference.

For a while, I placed my faith in effective altruism. Corin introduced me to the movement, as Swedish president. My partner was a fan. I met Kyran at an event in Melbourne. We spent an afternoon talking philosophy, then found out we worked from the same café. He was building a green-tech startup, with crazy levels of ambition. Friendship and collaboration moved fast, from editorial support, to culture building, to COO. What's more inclusive than sustainable energy grids? I decided to finish off other projects, and move to that startup full-time. Incidentally, there was a lot of money on the table, which could fund the Marco Polo Project, and the governance innovation work, and distributed public goods, down the track. Maybe the paths would converge again?

Except COVID-19 derailed everything. Ironically, pandemics were part of the black box I looked into when I worked on global catastrophic risk, and I was well aware of system collapse. It didn't make me any less vulnerable. Early 2020 was my point of biggest personal stretch: I was finishing a book manuscript, and a PhD, and exiting a charity, and starting full-time work on a startup. I needed optimal circumstances to pull through. Tough luck. The startup was the worst hit though. I will never know if claims of investors lining up were exaggerated, or if it all turned sour with COVID. We tried appealing to our local representative, so we could get on the government "JobKeeper" scheme, but pre-revenue ventures were not eligible – "the government sees it as a bunch of young people in their garage," I read in a paper at the time. No funding meant no progress, the team collapsed, and I left after six months. I had other responsibilities, and daily panic attacks, to take care of. Quitting wasn't enough to save the Marco Polo Project though. When government subsidies ended, the new CEO got another job. I encouraged him. With borders closed, our work was not sustainable, and we were all exhausted.

Innovation fails, generally: that's entrepreneurship 101. Yet every time I heard anyone talk about failure, they reframed it as "actually success" Sure, good things came out of the work I led, friendships blossomed, ideas and practices will be carried forward. Sure, I learned from it all, and I'll be fine. I have skills, experience, and networks. I completed my PhD, the crazy book project with Corin is close to done. I'm even returning to writing fiction (it's a romantic comedy on climate change). I'll join other projects, and communities – I already have. Yet I feel sad, angry, and disappointed, at myself and the world, for letting the Marco Polo Project collapse, for letting go of that green tech startup, for failing to keep hold of all those various threads. I feel a deep sense of loneliness, too, as if I was the only try-hard whose failure has nuggets of "not-actually-success." I feel cheated of a story that would make sense of what I attempted to do, and did. Which is why I am writing this: in the wild hope of finding common ground in failure that – in part – is only that. What's more inclusive, after all, than dreaming of a better world, falling short of creating it, but staying alive to keep trying.

challenges. However, inclusive innovation can be difficult to operationalize in practice, and so, challenges arise when deciding which activities "count." The policy imperative is then clear: at the outset it is essential to ensure shared understandings – across stakeholders in the ecosystem – of how to conceptualize inclusive innovation and agree what it looks like in practice.

Notes

1 Chris Oestereich and Kah Wei Yoong, *Green Growth: Zero Baht Shop*. UNESCAP Case Study. August 2018. https://sdghelpdesk.unescap.org/sites/default/files/2018-08/GG%20-%20Zero%20Baht%20Shop.pdf.

2 SCG, "Where waste keeps people alive." March 27, 2020. www.scg.com/sustainability/circular-economy/en/global-thailand-practices/on-nut-14-rai-community/.
3 Pierre Bourdieu, "The forms of capital." *Handbook of Theory and Research for the Sociology of Education*, J.G. Richardson (ed) (Westport, CT: Greenwood, 1986), 241–258; James S. Coleman, *Foundations of Social Theory* (Cambridge, MA: Harvard University Press, 1998); Alejandro Portes, "Social capital: its origins and applications in modern sociology." *Annual Review of Sociology* 24 (1998): 1–24.
4 Putnam, Robert D., *Making Democracy Work: Civic Traditions in Modern Italy* (Princeton: Princeton University Press, 1993), 35.
5 Klingler-Vidra and Liu, "Inclusive innovation policy as social capital accumulation strategy," 1034.
6 See Bourdieu, "The forms of capital," for a conceptualization of types of capital.
7 Niccolo Durrazi and Leonard Geyer, "Social inclusion in the knowledge economy: unions' strategies and institutional change in the Austrian and German training systems." *Socio-Economic Review* 18, no. 1 (2020): 103–124; Gerd Schienstock, "Social exclusion in the learning economy" in *The Globalizing Learning Economy,* Daniele Archibugi and Bengt-Åke Lundvall (eds) (Oxford: Oxford University Press, 2001).
8 Semih Akçomak and Bas ter Weel, "Social capital, innovation and growth: evidence from Europe." *Economic European Review* 53, no. 5 (2009): 551.
9 Yael Levitte, "Bonding social capital in entrepreneurial developing communities – survival networks or barriers?" *Journal of the Community Development Society* 35, no. 1 (2009): 45.
10 Mathijs De Vaan, Koen Frenken, and Ron Boschma, "The downside of social capital in new industry creation." *Economic Geography* 95, no. 4 (2019): 319.
11 Not that design thinking is ubiquitous across all inclusive innovation approaches. It can be a feature, but also, and as discussed elsewhere, inclusive innovation can be the result of complex adaptive system behavior of agents in the local context. Thanks to Elizabeth Hoffecker for this important point.
12 Ezio Manzini, *Design, When Everybody Designs: An Introduction to Design for Social Innovation* (Cambridge: MIT Press, 2015).
13 A "unicorn" is a privately-owned company with a value of US$ 1 billion or more.
14 Alex Ryan, "5 ways cities can drive sustainable innovation." *Smart Cities Dive.* September 11, 2019. www.smartcitiesdive.com/news/5-ways-cities-can-drive-sustainable-innovation/562531/.
15 Courtney Savie Lawrence, "Why the next generation of designers will save the world." *Design Management Review* 25, no. 2 (2014).
16 Ashley Westerman, "Should rivers have same legal rights as humans? A growing www.npr.org/2019/08/03/740604142/should-rivers-have-same-legal-rights-as-humans-a-growing-number-of-voices-say-ye?t=1626709474419.
17 Courtney Savie Lawrence, "From grassroots to government – why #inclusiveinnovation needs a stage." *Medium.* October 5, 2019. https://medium.com/@courtneysavie/from-grassroots-to-government-why-inclusiveinnovation-needs-a-stage-d2653b031172.
18 Mokter Hossain, "Grassroots innovation: A systematic review of two decades of research." *Journal of Cleaner Production* 137, no. 20 (2016): 973–981.
19 Janina Grabs, Nina Langen, Gesa Maschkowski, and Niko Schäpke, "Understanding role models for change: a multilevel analysis of success factors of

grassroots initiatives for sustainable consumption." *Journal of Cleaner Production* 134, Part A (2016): 98–111.

20 Dey and Gupta, "Policies and strategies to promote grassroots innovation workbook."

21 Eduardo Gustale, "Helping small go big; mainstreaming what happens in the margins." *UNDP Global Accelerator Labs*. February 12, 2021. www.undp.org/blogs/helping-small-go-big-mainstreaming-what-happens-margins

22 Anil K. Gupta, "Tapping the entrepreneurial potential of grassroots innovation." *Stanford Social Innovation Review* (Summer 2013).

23 Dey and Gupta, "Policies and strategies to promote grassroots innovation workbook."

24 Giuseppe Feola and Richard Joseph Nunes, "Success and failure of grassroots innovations for addressing climate change: the case of the transition movement." *Global Environmental Change* 24 (2014): 232–250.

25 Philippines Department of Science and Technology, Region XI, "DOST XI, UNDP Philippines conduct 'Saliklakbay' solutions mapping adventure." March 17, 2020. https://region11.dost.gov.ph/654-dost-xi-undp-philippines-conduct-saliklakbay-solutions-mapping-adventure.

26 Mulgan, Tucker, Ali, and Sanders, "Social innovation."

27 Tessa Morris-Suzuki and Eun Jeong Soh, "Social innovation in Asia: trends and characteristics in China, Korea, India, Japan and Thailand" in *New Worlds from Below: Informal Life Politics and Grassroots Action in Twenty-First Century Northeast Asia* (Canberra: Australian National University (ANU) Press, 2017), 249–274.

28 James A. Phills, Kriss Deiglmeier, and Dale T. Miller, "Rediscovering social innovation." *Stanford Social Innovation Review* (Fall 2008).

29 Peter Oeij, Wouter van der Torre, Fietje Vaas, and Steven Dhondt, "Understanding social innovation as an innovation process: applying the innovation journey model." *Journal of Business Research* 101, no. 8 (2019): 244.

30 Monica E. Edwards-Schachter, Cristian E. Matti, and Enrique Alcántara, "Fostering quality of life through social innovation: a living lab methodology study case." *Review of Policy Research* 29, no. 6 (2012): 679–680.

31 Van der Have, Robert P., and Lius Rubalcaba, "Social innovation research: an emerging area of innovation studies?" *Research Policy* 45, no. 9 (2016): 1923–1935.

32 For an overview of social innovation in East Asia, see Dangshu (Jaff) Shen and Fan Li, "East Asia's role in global social innovation." *Stanford Social Innovation Review*. February 16, 2017.

33 Rafael Ziegler, "Social innovation as a collaborative concept." *Innovation: The European Journal of Social Science Research* 30, no. 4 (2017): 388–405.

34 Carolyn Curtis, Chris Vanstone, and Melanie Rayment, "Social R&D: a new way to accelerate progress on tough social challenges." *The Australian Centre for Social Innovation*. June 2021. https://tacsi.org.au/wp-content/uploads/2021/06/TACSI-Social-RandD.pdf.

35 Aisling Irwin, "No PhDs needed: how citizen science is transforming research." *Nature*. October 23, 2018. www.nature.com/articles/d41586-018-07106-5.

36 Geoff Mulgan, "The process of social innovation." *Innovations: Technology, Governance, Globalization* 1 no. 2 (2006): 145–162.

37 Geoff Mulgan and Charles Leadbeater, "Systems innovation. Discussion paper." *Nesta*. January 2013, p. 7. https://media.nesta.org.uk/documentssystems_innovation_discussion_paper.pdf.

38 Frank W. Geels, Benjamin K. Sovacool, Tim Schwanen, and Steve Sorrell, "Sociotechnical transitions for deep decarbonization." *Science*, 357, no. 6357 (2017): 1242–1244.

39 Odin Mühlenbein, "Systems change – big or small?" *Stanford Social Innovation Review*. February 5, 2018. https://ssir.org/articles/entry/systems_changebig_or_small#.

40 Leadbetter and Winhall, "Building better systems," 8.

41 Dominic Hofstetter, "Innovating in complexity (Part II): from single-point solutions to directional systems innovation." *Medium*. July 26, 2019. https://medium.com/in-search-of-leverage/innovating-in-complexity-part-ii-from-single-point-solutions-to-directional-systems-innovation-dfb36fcfe50.

42 Petrarca Karetji, "Towards collaborative and interconnected innovations: development as an ecosystem." *Medium*. July 6, 2021. https://medium.com/pulse-lab-jakarta/towards-collaborative-and-interconnected-innovations-development-as-an-ecosystem-f38c55ba1c2c.

43 They are active in action research, publishing, and report-making, provide and hold roundtables and workshops, work to create strategies and action plans that sustain change, and are involved in project management with various actors. In addition, they provide mentorship, training, and team-building activities. WeSolve has been involved in seven projects: (1) #MoveAsOne, (2) Responding to the Scandal of Invisibility through Better Birth Registration, (3) Private Sector Involvement in the SDGs, (4) Data for Empowerment (Quality Data), (5) Provincial Health and COVID-19, (6) Budget Tracking and Accountability, and (7) Building a future-proof circular food system for Metro Manila. The projects are inclusive of innovators, whether this includes volunteers, civil society, or NGOs that serve the needs of their beneficiaries.

44 Geels, Sovacool, Schwanen, and Sorrell, "Sociotechnical transitions for deep decarbonization," 4.

45 Will Steffen, Johan Rockström, Katherine Richardson, Timothy M. Lenton, Carl Folke, Diana Liverman, Colin P. Summerhayes, Anthony D. Barnosky, Sarah E. Cornell, Michel Crucifix, Jonathan F. Donges, Ingo Fetzer, Steven J. Lade, Marten Scheffer, Ricarda Winkelmann, and Hans Joachim Schellnhuber, "Trajectories of the earth system in the anthropocene." *Proceedings of the National Academy of Sciences in the United States of America* 115, no. 33 (2018): 8252–8259.

46 Sandra Waddock and Steve Wadell, "Transformation catalysts: weaving transformational change for a flourishing world for all." *Cadmus Journal* 4, no. 1 (2021): 165–182.

47 See Chris Argyris, "Single-loop and double-loop models in research on decision making." *Administrative Science Quarterly* 21 no. 3 (1976): 363–376; Paul Tosey, Max Visser, and Mark N.K. Saunders, "The origins and conceptualizations of 'triple-loop' learning: a critical review." *Management Learning* 43, no. 3 (2012): 291–307.

48 Catrien J.A.M. Termeer, Art Dewulf, and G. Robert Biesbroek, "Transformational change: governance interventions for climate change adaptation from a continuous change perspective." *Journal of Environmental Planning and Management* 60, no. 4 (2017): 558–576.

49 Ana Maria Peredo and Murdith McLean, "Social entrepreneurship: a critical review of the concept." *Journal of World Business* 41, no. 1 (2006): 56–65.

50 Michael P. Schlaile, Sophie Urmetzer, Marcus B. Ehrenberger, and Joe Brewer, "Systems entrepreneurship: a conceptual substantiation of a novel entrepreneurial 'species.'" *Sustainability Science* 16 (2021): 786–787.

51 Martin and Osberg, "Social entrepreneurship." Shahriar Akter, Nabila Jamal, Md Mahfuz Ashraf, Grace McCarthy, and P.S. Varsha, "The rise of the social business in emerging economies: a new paradigm of development." *Journal of Social Entrepreneurship* 11, no. 3 (2020): 282–299; Michael H. Morris, Susana C. Santos, and Donald F. Kuratko, "The great divides in social entrepreneurship and where they lead us." *Small Business Economics* 54, no. 2 (2020).

52 Schlaile, Urmetzer, Ehrenberger, and Brewer, "Systems entrepreneurship."

53 Nitin Nohria, Michael Beer, and Nitin Nohria, *Cracking the Code of Change. Harvard Business Review.* May–June 2000. https://hbr.org/2000/05/cracking-the-code-of-change.

54 Charles Edquist and Bjorn Johnson, "Institutions and organizations in systems of innovation" in (ed) *Systems of Innovation: Technologies, Institutions, and Organizations,* Charles Edquist (ed) (London: Pinter, 1997), 41–63.

55 Knox and Tan, "For regenerative impact."

56 Daniela Papi-Thornton, "Tackling heropreneurship." *Stanford Social Innovation Review.* February 23, 2016. https://ssir.org/articles/entry/tackling_heropreneurship#.

57 For a full list of partner institutions and research outputs, see www.seasin-eu.org/sisus/.

58 See https://ateneo.edu/sites/default/files/Project%20Brief%20-%20UNIID-SEA.pdf for the overview.

59 The Asia Foundation, "Civil society in Southeast Asia during COVID-19: responding and evolving under pressure." *GovAsia* 1 (September 2020). https://asiafoundation.org/wp-content/uploads/2020/09/GovAsia-1.1-Civil-society-in-Southeast-Asia-during-the-COVID-19-pandemic.pdf.

60 See https://catalyst2030.net for more.

61 Ekin Alakent, M. Sinan Goktan, and Theodore A. Khoury, "Is venture capital socially responsible? Exploring the imprinting effect of VC funding on CSR practices." *Journal of Business Venturing* 35, no. 3 (2020): 106005.

62 Steve Waddell, *An Investigation into Financing Transformation.* Catalyst 2030. June 2021, p. 11. https://catalyst2030.net/resources/an-investigation-into-financing-transformation/.

63 Caitlin Wiesen, Ida Uusikyla, Morgane Rivoal, Le Thi Thu Hien, Bui Hoa Binh, Nguyen Tuan Luong, Phan Hoang Lan, and Alex Oprunenco, "What would a circular economic rebound mean for Vietnam?" *Medium, UNDP Innovation.* June 30, 2021. https://medium.com/@undp.innovation/what-would-a-circular-economic-rebound-mean-for-viet-nam-dbd279619c03.

64 Waddell, *An Investigation into Financing Transformation.*

65 C40 Cities, *C40 Mayors' Agenda for a Green and Just Recovery.* Policy Brief. July 2020. www.c40knowledgehub.org/s/article/C40-Mayors-Agenda-for-a-Green-and-Just-Recovery?language=en_US.

66 The Zero Gap Fund, by the Rockefeller Foundation, sources, funds, and develops innovative financial solutions that demonstrate the potential to catalyze large-scale private investment towards the SDGs; it was launched in partnership with the John D. and Catherine T. MacArthur Foundation through the Catalytic Capital Consortium (C3) to fund the world's urgent challenges. For more, see the

Rockefeller Foundation, "Zero gap fund: state of the portfolio." July 12, 2021. www.rockefellerfoundation.org/wp-content/uploads/2021/07/Zero-Gap-Fund-Annual-Report-2020-External.pdf

67 See https://asiafoundation.org/wp-content/uploads/2021/07/Coalitions-for-Cha nge-Program-overview_2021.pdf.

68 For more on the Thai approaches, www.nxpo.or.th/th/en/foresight-and-system-research.

69 Nesta, "Anticipatory regulation." October 12, 2021. www.nesta.org.uk/feature/innovation-methods/anticipatory-regulation/.

70 Ishtiaque Hussain and Vichet Seat, "Inclusive public service innovation in Cambodia: taking a systems view." *UNDP Cambodia.* June 4, 2020. www.kh.undp.org/content/cambodia/en/home/blog/inclusive-public-service-innovation-in-cambodia--taking-a-system.html.

71 Philippines Senate, "An act institutionalizing the poverty reduction through social entrepreneurship (PRESENT) program and promoting social enterprises with the poor as primary stakeholders." July 2019.

72 Robyn Klingler-Vidra and Rex Lor, "Bringing the environment back into our understanding of inclusive innovation." *UNDP Philippines.* May 20, 2021. www.ph.undp.org/content/philippines/en/home/blog/bringing-the-environment-back-into-our-understanding-of-inclusiv.html.

73 Papaioannou, "How inclusive can innovation and development be in the twenty-first century?"

74 Dey and Gupta, "Policies and strategies to promote grassroots innovation workbook." *UNESCAP.* August 2020.

75 GALI, *Does Acceleration Work?* May 2021. www.galidata.org/assets/report/pdf/Does%20Acceleration%20Work_EN.pdf.

76 See the Impact Hub guide to gender lens acceleration https://genderlensaccelerat ion.impacthub.net/ and the "Gender lens incubation and acceleration toolkit." https://toolkits.scalingfrontierinnovation.org/wp-content/uploads/2019/12/FrontierIncubator_ToolkitPDF.pdf

77 Knox and Tan, "For regenerative impact."

78 John Elkington, *Cannibals with Forks* (Oxford: Capstone, 2002).

79 Malik Mahfuja, "Value-enhancing capabilities of CSR: a brief review of contemporary literature." *Journal of Business Ethics* 127 no. 2 (2015): 425.

80 Colin Mayer, *Firm Commitment: Why the Corporation Is Failing Us and How to Restore Trust in It* (Oxford: Oxford University Press, 2013).

81 Michael E. Porter and Mark R. Kramer, "Creating shared value." *Harvard Business Review.* January–February 2011.

82 The rise of sustainability in consumer preferences is something that is altering the competitive considerations of established firms. McGrath (2013) uses the term "transient advantage" to refer to the way in which a firm's relative advantage is fleeting. This notion of changing advantage over time is pertinent here, as a financially sustainable business model is increasingly coinciding with environmentally and socially sustainable practices.

83 C.K. Prahalad, *The Fortune at the Bottom of the Pyramid: Eradicating Poverty through Profits* (Chennai: Pearson Education India, 2009); Deepa Prahalad, "The new fortune at the bottom of the pyramid." *Strategy & Business.* January 2, 2019. www.strategy-business.com/article/The-New-Fortune-at-the-Bottom-of-the-Pyramid?gko=c5f11.

84 Christina Gradl and Beth Jenkins, *Tackling Barriers to Scale: From Inclusive Business Models to Inclusive Business Ecosystems* (Cambridge, MA: Harvard Kennedy School, 2011).

85 Robin Hicks, "Sustainable business certifier B Corp is launching in Southeast Asia." *Eco-Business.* June 2, 2021. www.eco-business.com/news/sustainable-business-certifier-b-corp-is-launching-in-southeast-asia/.

86 Robyn Klingler-Vidra and Robert H. Wade, "Science and technology policies and the middle income trap: lessons from Vietnam." *Journal of Development Studies* 56, no. 4 (2020): 717–731.

87 World Bank, *Vietnam Inclusive Innovation (P121643) Implementation Completion Report (ICR) Review,* 1.

88 World Bank, *Vietnam Inclusive Innovation (P121643) Implementation Completion Report (ICR) Review,* 3.

89 World Bank, *Vietnam Inclusive Innovation (P121643) Implementation Completion Report (ICR) Review.* November 30, 2018. https://documents1.worldbank.org/curated/en/308921530293865449/pdf/Vietnam-Vietnam-Inclusive-Innovation.pdf.

3 What

Innovation for environmental and social good

This chapter explores technology-supported innovations addressing economic, environmental and social challenges. Such "technology for good" approaches have been developed to tackle issues in a variety of arenas, including waste collection, education provision, low incomes in the agricultural sector, and infrastructure issues facing excluded groups. The unifying feature is that such initiatives assume that technology – as the "what" – is central to fostering a just equilibrium.

Our exploration begins with the reasons behind why technology would not naturally address complex societal or environmental challenges. For example, in a 2019 UNCTAD article on the relationship between technology and development, Shamika Sirimanne observed that:

> arguably one of the most transformative technological developments of our time – artificial intelligence – could be used to help identify solutions to our most intractable economic, social and environmental challenges. However, its applications in public and private sectors could counterintuitively scale inequality and make the world less secure.[1]

As this quote asserts, technology can introduce, rather than reduce, societal challenges. Aghion et al. explain that "governmental intervention is necessary to incentivize these firms to redirect their innovative activity from polluting technologies to green technologies."[2] Without external incentives, they contend, radically different technologies, such as green technologies, will not naturally proliferate (Table 3.1).

The Economist, for instance, showcased examples of medical innovations – such as pulse oximeters – that do not properly work for people with non–white skin tones.[3] This, they note, can have potentially fatal consequences, as medical diagnoses are inaccurate, and so treatment does not follow as it should. This, as well as the potential for more creative outputs, is the basis of the case for a more diverse set of individuals in the production of technologically-supported innovation.[4] As another example, the disproportionate power of technology companies emanating from elsewhere can have a negative impact on local environs in Southeast Asia. Facebook, for instance, was found

DOI: 10.4324/9781003125877-3

Table 3.1 What: key concepts and sections

Key concepts	AI; automation technology; EdTech; green technology; Luddite movement; Schumpeterian innovation; technological unemployment; technology for good; waste management
Sections	What are the technologies for environmental and social good? What are appropriate technologies? What technological advance can displace labor? What technologies can bring jobs? Who is involved in this approach, and how? Strengths and shortcomings.

guilty of being used to incite genocide in Myanmar,[5] and the October 2021 WhatsApp outage caused damage throughout the region, for the millions who depend on the platform in order to communicate with family, friends, customers, and suppliers.

Some inclusive innovators use technology as a means of enhancing conditions and opportunities for workers with lower incomes, rather than automating the services they provide. For instance, RecyGlo uses its technology platform to connect local waste collectors in Myanmar to domestic and international waste buyers, rather than cutting them out of the value chain. RecyGlo is a Myanmar-based startup that seeks to develop solutions to waste management and recycling. It started as an "Uber for recycling" and has expanded to provide services such as training to businesses and households on how to separate waste and recycle, as well as logistics and traceability solutions for waste management. RecyGlo's founder, Okka Maung, told us that:

> Yangon's municipal government tries, but they can only serve a quarter of the eight million people who live here. Lots of waste goes to landfill, which is bad for the environment and results in pollution.

He went on to observe that "this sector is not fancy and it is not easy to make a lot of money in a short time, but it is a long-term game." He believes that RecyGlo's technology-enabled circular economy approach is a long-term game worthy of his effort and ingenuity.

Other initiatives emphasize the need to bring marginalized groups in as producers of innovation, helping to quell inequality by widening access to technological employment. An example of this approach is a Vietnamese software startup called Enablecode, which is employing and training disabled people to work as freelance developers, coders, web designers, and experts in artificial intelligence (AI) business processes. As Enablecode's CEO Colin Blackwell told us, "People can work in technology without having to have technological backgrounds." The concept and founding of Enablecode came about when the founders, Colin Blackwell and Paul Bapoo, noticed that there were very few disabled people who had academic training or qualifications for jobs in the knowledge economy.

The Enablecode team provides training so that disabled people in Vietnam are able to help code high-quality web and mobile app development, as well as digital marketing support, to clients all over the world. According to the founders, the ideal workers in this type of technological application need to be good at problem-solving and have tacit knowledge. By facing adversity in their everyday lives, the problem-solving abilities of disabled people are strong. In a creative, collaborative environment they could provide clever, innovative solutions to their clients' software development needs. Enablecode's vision sought to transform the way Vietnamese society perceives disabled people through employment at the technological frontier (specifically, AI).

RecyGlo and Enablecode are examples of inclusive innovation that harnesses technology as the "what" to drive societal and environmental change: either to boost the participation in the production of innovation (e.g. Enablecode), or to ameliorate innovation's tendency to accentuate inequality by advancing technological innovation for an underserved set of consumers (e.g. RecyGlo).

What are technologies for environmental and social good?

The language of "tech for good," and the movement surrounding it, has emerged within the past decade. The premise is that technology is not inherently good or bad, it's the direction that determines the impact it has on society and the environment. This fits closely with our approach, and that of Nesta's focus on the "direction" of innovation, in order to determine its inclusiveness.[6] Tech for good, as detailed by the McKinsey Global Institute, includes six major themes on which technology can help to address complex challenges: (1) job security, (2) material living standards, (3) health and longevity, (4) education, (5) environmental sustainability, and (6) equal opportunities.[7] A related concept – "digital for good" – takes a similar tack, in advocating the case for conceiving for the socially positive uses of technology, especially in terms of its applications in education.[8]

The advance of technology allows us to develop solutions to address environmental problems. High-tech, AI, and alternative energy sources have the potential to promote global sustainability, tackling problems such as global warming, climate change, and an increase in radiation waste. In the spirit of intersectionality, agricultural productivity – leading to improvements in living standards for farmers – and sustainability can both benefit from the advance of solar technologies. As an example, supported by the World Bank's Second Rural Electrification and Renewable Energy Development Project, a growing number of farmers are installing solar power irrigation pumps, which are not only more reliable, but also cleaner and less expensive than diesel or conventional electric pumps.[9] In Vietnam, high-tech agricultural parks strive to simultaneously improve local livelihoods and environmental practices related to farming.[10]

An example of technological development in order to improve both the access to, and quality of, education systems – the fourth pillar in the McKinsey list of Tech for Good fields – in Southeast Asia is 360ed in Myanmar, as detailed in Box 3.1.

Box 3.1 360ed

In Myanmar, education has traditionally focused on rote learning or memorization. Many schools lacked models and experimental installations for science education. That conventional way of learning and teaching is tedious not only for students but also for teachers. Hla Hla Win, a former elementary teacher who studied her first degree in K-12 education and completed a Master's degree in education policy and was inspired by taking part in a series of hackathons, aspired to reform Myanmar's education system. In 2016, with the vision of bringing Augmented Reality (AR) and Virtual Reality (VR) tools and products into Myanmar schools, Hla Hla Win launched 360ed, an education tech startup. "AR and VR technology is creative and highly advanced. I thought I could help reform our country's education system by using it," said Hla Hla Win in an interview with the *Myanmar Times*.[11]

Most of the company's products use so-called "Dat Thin Pone" (digital tablets), which offers a more exciting and engaging way for students to learn science, math, and languages via apps and flashcards. "We do not want to replace the teachers with technology but upgrade their abilities to create a culture of self-learning confidence," said Hla Hla Win in an interview with us in 2019. Indeed, rural schools in Myanmar have struggled to acquire and retain talented teachers. 360ed provides low-cost tools built around traditional texts and textbooks in flashcard form and matches them with AR on low-cost smartphones using mobile or Wi-Fi. Therefore, they can provide first-rate science education any-where and everywhere. In so doing, the teacher migrates from the all-knowing lecturer to the co-learning specialist guiding students through automated software and textbook programs.

For Hla Hla Win, inclusive education is finding ways to involve all students and supporting teachers to teach in innovative ways that connect with different kinds of learning and encourage critical thinking and soft skills. She wants 360ed to be part of building the nation in Myanmar. In order to grow a knowledge-based education system, she asserts that a trisectoral partnership between the public sector, private sector, and civil society/UN agencies is needed. In this vein, 360ed has been working closely with the Ministry of Education to support the delivery of the National Education Strategic Plan and has provided support to UNESCO, who delivered preservice teacher training reform on behalf of the Ministry of Education.

Nevertheless, switching from a long-standing method of education to a new one requires a lot of time, and the process is not without challenges. Hla Hla Win shared with us four key challenges her company encounters:

1. Absence of a legal framework for a company to be registered as a social enterprise and lacking a support system and incentives to support their development.
2. Lifeline of tech companies is the protection of Intellectual Property Rights. Unfortunately, Myanmar's legal system is not mature enough to give such companies enough protection to thrive.
3. There are practical challenges, for example, around connectivity and access – 360ed had to start with offline apps and tested their products in camps for internally displaced persons (IDPs) to see how they could make them accessible to people without regular internet access.
4. Access to finance – banks will not give loans as tech companies do not belong to the SME category, and banks do not have a framework to evaluate and give seed money.

In Myanmar, startups like 360ed that use digital technology to address societal challenges are increasing in number and scale. 360ed shows that startups can change society with their entrepreneurial spirit and that financing partners and support from external partners are essential for them to thrive and ultimately achieve their goals.

360ed uses ICT tools to drive wider access to high-quality STEM education across Myanmar. Tech for good is, though, not necessarily ICT-focused. For example, in 2001, the "Pot-in-Pot" – an invention of Mohammed Bah Abba, a Nigerian potter, was named invention of the year by *Time* magazine.[12] His invention is sometimes called the "desert refrigerator" and it works very simply: one pot sits inside another, and damp sand fills the space in between. As the sand dries in the desert air, heat in the inner pot is wicked away, keeping the contents cool. Therefore, farmers no longer have to rush selling because of spoilage.

In another arena, research has shown how governance, and the livelihood of citizens, can benefit if technology is oriented for good. For instance, the proliferation of big data in the form of satellite images and cell phone data are increasingly shedding light on various socioeconomic parameters.[13] Such a use of AI technology can help identify needs in order to develop appropriate strategies. Given the ubiquity of online platforms, there are also further opportunities to digitally engage citizens. However, not all citizens can equally access digital services. *The Economist* profiles how high-technology government services, such as those offered in India, are actually accessible only to a very small share of the population, worsening the implications of the digital divide.[14] "Govnepreneurs" – entrepreneurs within the government – such as Anir Chowdhury at a2i in Bangladesh are working to develop digital platforms so that they reach wider society. See Ishtiaque Hussain's story, as detailed in Box 3.6 at the end of this chapter for more on Digital Bangladesh.

In a similar manner, emerging technologies such as 3D printing can offer socially good solutions, and there is initial application of this technology with the aim of addressing environmental and societal challenges. For instance, 3D printing has found applications in the context of vision impairment. According to the World Health Organization, at least 2.2 billion people in the world are visually impaired, with the prevalence of distance vision impairment in low- and middle-income regions estimated to be four times higher than in high-income regions.[15] Visually impaired individuals in socioeconomically disadvantaged areas may not be given the right treatment because of fragile frames, high costs, and variations required in frame design. With 3D printing technology, self-adjustable eyeglasses can be manufactured to create ideal and sustainable glasses.[16] The use of 3D printing technologies aligns well with technology for good as it offers the pursuit of distributed place-based innovation as well as waste reduction in the production process.[17] With 3D printing, goods transportation, and reliance on wider supply chains, are reduced.

Tech for good is also pertinent in the context of *accessible* technology and *assistive* technology.[18] Access to information and basic technology such as computers is more essential than ever in employment, education, and daily life, but the high cost of such technologies is putting the assistive technology out of reach of people with low incomes. The problem is particularly acute for disabled people. Special interface technology may be necessary but has, as of yet, not been provided widely.[19] Therefore, to promote equality, the direction of technology would be to ensure that everyone can access it regardless of abilities. When deployed, technology can transform the lives of millions, especially of the marginalized and vulnerable groups: the DMap app offers real-time information on accessibility and mobility for a range of buildings and public spaces in Vietnam. In Southeast Asia, social enterprises are working to both develop technological solutions for disabled people and to raise awareness,[20] as Box 3.2 shows in the case of DRD's DMap in Vietnam.

Tech for environmental good, often referred to as "green tech", refers to technologies that are integrated with environmental practices, thereby providing a sustainable solution to prevent degradation and depletion of environmental and natural resources. Tech for socioeconomic good can also aim to

---

Box 3.2 DMap: innovation for mobility inclusion

By ThS. Nguyễn Thanh Tùn, Disability Research and Capacity Development (DRD)

The Vietnamese Convention on the Rights of Persons with Disabilities in 2014 led to the enactment of the Law on People with Disabilities and created a national construction code to ensure disabled people can access public sites. However, many construction and transport sites throughout the country, including in large cities like Hanoi and Ho Chi Minh City, still fail to meet the code, and so remain difficult to access. Rather than waiting for the reality to match the code, Dr. Vo T. Hoang Yen launched DMap (Disability Map), a smart phone app that aims to help disabled people to find information on accessible infrastructures in Vietnam. At the DMap launch event, Dr. Vo, founder and director of Ho Chi Minh City-based NGO, DRD, and vice-chairwomen of the Vietnam Federation for Disabilities, shared a story of disabled students who could not use their school's toilets for 12 years because the doors were too narrow for a wheelchair to enter. Dr. Vo herself started to use crutches when she was three years old and has been in a wheelchair since 2010.

In an interview in August 2019, Dr. Vo explained that "we developed DMap, so we have more information about accessible places, and the aim is to raise awareness of the inaccessibility of Vietnam." DMap collects information about accessible public infrastructures so that people can use the app to know the locations of disability-friendly community venues and public sites. DMap spans a range of spaces and building types, such as parks, offices, restaurants, and so forth, each of which is essential in daily life for everybody.

In the long term, Dr. Vo and the team strive to raise public awareness about the need for inclusion of disabled people in society. They hope to achieve this by making accessibility issues more mainstream, and having more data on mobility and accessibility challenges. At the time of our interview, the Dmap database contained information on roughly 18,171 places and had reached around 1,332 users. The ultimate goal is to build a database of at least 15,000 public places, including restaurants, shopping malls, entertainment centers, and religious buildings.

---

improve agricultural productivity and local livelihoods. We consider green tech in four areas: energy, climate, access to clean water, and waste management.

Technology for good has been hailed in the context of energy access and quality. One of the motivating issues – or unjust equilibria – is that rural areas can have limited access to modern energy services due to problems of availability and affordability. At the same time, relying on conventional fuels is not an ideal option. Research has shown that exposure to indoor air pollution from the combustion of solid fuels has been implicated as a causal agent of several diseases in developing countries.[21] Increasing access to technologies that use modern fuels or make use of traditional fuels in cleaner, safer, and more environmentally sound ways, and extended access to electricity through alternative resources such as wind or solar is needed. Renewable energy technologies have immense potential to meet the energy needs of rural societies in a sustainable way, and the decentralized nature of some such technologies allows them to be matched with the specific needs of different rural areas.[22]

In a similar way, tech for good in the context of the climate has the potential to achieve reductions in global greenhouse gas emissions.[23] This can be achieved by creating linkages. The logic follows that when demand for energy across sectors of the economy is reduced, there will be less demand for fossil fuels, hence lessening the hurdles for transitioning to renewable energy. NASA's support offers an illustrative example. NASA supports scientists monitoring conditions on the ground and in the oceans and atmosphere, including innovative devices, such as its Orbiting Carbon Observatory satellite launched in 2014, to study local greenhouse gases and ocean conditions. Resulting data aids the process of verifying and enriching NASA's model of Earth's weather and climate, which span decades, and peer into the future.[24]

Tech for good is also emerging in the context of tackling the problem of access to clean water. Desalination technology is particularly useful in regions such as remote islands or where building desalination plants is not feasible. Similarly, to alleviate the water scarcity in arid regions, a team of researchers from the Massachusetts Institute of Technology (MIT) and the University of California Berkeley has designed a passive system that extracts water from dry air by consuming only solar energy.[25] Access to clean water through such innovative water tech solutions is promising.

In a related domain, tech for good has advanced waste management solutions. The world generates an excessive amount of garbage every year, and according to a World Bank report, at least 33 percent of that is not managed in an environmentally-safe manner.[26] Recycling cannot be the sole solution for this problem as there is a wide gap between what is possible to recycle and what actually is recycled. Tech companies have also designed multidirectional approaches to tackle the problem. For example, AMP Robotics, a startup founded by Matanya Horowitz, offers solutions to some of the recycling industry's biggest challenges with AI and machine vision based autonomous recyclables-sorting technologies:

> If you reduce the cost of sorting, the margin you can extract on all those materials increases and you naturally find an incentive to capture that material. That's precisely what our technology does, and how we go about our mission of enabling a world without waste.[27]

Another approach was designed to use technology to reduce how much plastic waste is even produced. Avantium, a Dutch company, has been producing plant-based plastic that is made entirely from feedstocks, ensuring that the material is fully recyclable and degradable.[28]

Tech for good was also evident in the myriad responses to the COVID-19 pandemic. To organize and support technologies that were addressing social challenges caused by the pandemic, and related lockdowns, UNDP Vietnam organized a hackathon in April 2020, which serves as a good example of tech for good. See Box 3.3 for more on Hack Co Vy.

Box 3.3 Hack Co Vy: innovating to hack COVID-19 in Vietnam

By Ida Uusikyla, UNDP Vietnam

In April 2020, UNDP Vietnam, in collaboration with the Ho Chi Minh Communist Youth Union and Angel Hack, ran the first-ever COVID-19 online hackathon in Vietnam: Hack Co Vy. As the name suggests, the hackathon was organized to offer a (digital) space for tech lovers and startups to come together to create innovative solutions to the urgent challenges caused by the pandemic. Hack Co Vy strived to offer an opportunity for the contestants to learn and develop themselves, to contribute to creating positive and sustainable social impact.

Hack Co Vy received over 420 registrations from all over the world, with more than 500 developers, entrepreneurs, and designers working in teams to develop 63+ technology-based projects. The teams had 48 hours to develop solutions in line with one of six areas within the framework of the UN SDGs: Economy, Education, Climate, Health, Inequality, and Governance.

The hackathon's finalists consisted of eight teams, each of them working to create sustainable solutions to tackle the complex challenges associated with the pandemic. The projects were assessed by 22 judges based on five criteria: (1) Simplicity, (2) Creativity, (3) Impact, (4) Design, and (5) Scalability. Three winners were announced for their respective category:

- Ideation track: DHSYN with the Quaranhome application, a system managing centralized quarantine facilities and supporting people in quarantine by providing up-to-date, accessible information.
- Acceleration track: AIOZ for their Beetle Bot project, which provides robots that can help doctors and administrators in hospitals by delivering medication and equipment.
- VinAI challenge: Mắm with their GudNews as a platform to minimize the circulation of Fake News.

Hack Co Vy 2020 was one of the first technology competitions in Vietnam that upholds the spirit of creativity for social impact, and in particular, in responding to an urgent societal challenge (COVID-19). The hackathon has helped to establish many new scalable ideas and partnerships and helped to lay the foundation for a stronger technology-focused inclusive innovator community across the country.

What are appropriate technologies?

In some ways, the tech for good is a contemporary version of the appropriate technologies (AT) movement's focus on the environmental and social opportunities and consequences of technological innovation. As mentioned in Chapter 1, seminal thinking about the relationship between technology and inclusion comes from the AT movement, which was crystalized in Schumacher's influential *Small Is Beautiful* book.[29] For Schumacher, the diffusion of advanced technologies serves as "poverty-reinforcing tools of much of the southern hemisphere."[30] The AT movement, which Schumacher's work typifies, is situated as a critique of the notion that exogenous technology, diffused from advanced economies, could sufficiently fit the demand and supply fundamentals in developing contexts. In this sense, the AT movement is distinct from tech for good, as it has global distributional concerns, and the prioritization of local context, as priorities for thinking about which types of technological innovation should be developed.

The AT movement was ideologically rooted in the desire to resist pressures towards large-scale, hegemonic, and masculine technologies. It offered a counter to the operating premise that aid programs should provide for technical assistance in order to advance developing countries' patterns of industrialization as experienced in advanced economies.[31] Such appropriate (sometimes called "intermediate") technologies were defined as:

(1) cheap enough to be accessible to nearly everyone, (2) simple enough to be easily maintained and repaired, (3) suitable for small-scale application, (4) compatible with man's needs for creativity, and (5) self-educative in environmental awareness.[32]

In his distilling of Schumacher's thinking about AT, Kaplinsky outlined similar attributes, as well as the case for their labor-intensive character and minimally-harmful environmental impact.[33] Different thinkers in the movement conceived of technologies that "could be considered 'appropriate' for that time and place," in terms of society *and* the environment.[34]

The primary concern for Schumacher and the AT movement is the consideration of technologies' contextual fit with the local community and environment, rather than the diffusion of so-called mainstream economic growth and related productivity advances to developing economies.

In contrast, Schumpeterian notions of innovation prioritize the advance of productivity, without placing distribution and the environment in core of the analytical lens.[35] For Schumpeter, innovative new entrants to a market trigger a process of creative destruction. Creative destruction – in which existing firms and technologies lose out to those new market forces – propels activity forward (e.g. creates new jobs, improves quality of life, and restructures the economy's wealth distribution). Wong et al. depict Schumpeter's "entrepreneurs as innovators" who are "causing constant disturbances to an economic system in equilibrium, creating opportunities for economic rent."[36]

Schumpeter noted that creative destruction, which serves as the essential motor of capitalism, would be met with resistance and resentment, as it creates and ruins fortunes.[37] While he contended that distributional concerns were an inevitable reaction to the gains and dislocations of creative destruction, he did not suggest dampening or redirecting the force. It was, rather, thinking of strategies by which capitalist benefits could ultimately overcoming pressures for redistribution. This is why Schumacher and the AT movement, which emphasize local context, distribution, and environmental fit rather than productivity advances, offer such a clear intellectual opposite to Schumpeter's view of the role of innovation.

An example of an appropriate technology, which accords with Schumacher's contention, comes from work done by social enterprises such as Proximity Designs in Myanmar. Proximity Designs works to apply contextually-relevant technologies to improve agricultural production. This often includes farmers and agricultural workers receiving advice and training from agronomists to enable continuous improvement through innovation. Efforts are also made to create stronger relationships between farmers and regional research and innovation centers, and amongst farmers themselves, to enable the sharing of knowledge and resources. This is essential to boosting both the output of agriculture and the livelihoods of farmers.

In the context of inclusive innovation, the approach taken by policymakers, entrepreneurs, and communities is to actively shape the *direction* of technological innovation, such that the advances are in areas that stand to address societal and environmental challenges. In doing so, they place Schumacher's environmental and socioeconomic aims alongside Schumpeter's narrower aims. They also work to adjust participation in innovative activities, so that technology-oriented employment opportunities are more widely available, particularly in demographic terms (e.g. age, disability status, ethnicity, gender, race, and sexuality). Featured in Box 3.4, Proximity Designs is an example of a startup developing AT for farmers.

Box 3.4 Proximity designs: appropriate technology for Myanmar's farmers

Jim Taylor and Debbie Aung Din launched Proximity Designs in 2004 with the commitment to create a social business for Myanmar's under-served rural families. Starting out as the first provider of micro-finance solutions for farmers in Myanmar, it has since expanded and become one of the most well-established agricultural services platforms in the country. They integrate technology into farming, thereby increasing productivity of the land while lowering the costs. Their Yetagon ("water-fall" in Burmese) products, which is what the Proximity team call their portfolio of AgTech products, are designed to replace the back-breaking and time-consuming work of hauling water from the well to the fields. The Yetagon products include the "mister," a rain device, the "red rhino," a mobile foot-powered water pump, and the Crop Protection Service, a diagnostic and treatment support for crop pests and diseases through on-farm and tele-agronomy.

Win Myint, an onion farmer in Moe Kaung village, in Myanmar's Dry Zone, was among one of the firsts to purchase Proximity Designs' drip system, and later the sprinkler system. Before installing the system in his farm, it cost him almost US$10 a day to water his plots. The dripping system cost him only US$31 and within the first three months, he was able to save US$80 to reinvest in his farm. Speaking of the impact of AT, Win Myint said, "my farming is more precise, and my soil is more balanced with the new sprinkler."

Overall, Proximity's services support Myanmar's family farms by delivering AT to boost – not replace – their agricultural production. As a social enterprise, Proximity considers those that it serves as customers – people who are owed empathy, not sympathy, and who expect a return on their investment and a say about the value they receive.

What technological advance can displace labor?

One of the central concerns about technological advance, in the context of inclusion, has to do with its ability to make jobs obsolete. Worries about the risks that technological advances pose to society are not new to the contemporary era. Concerns about automation's risk to society appeared prominently during the Industrial Revolution in the 18th century, as crafts people stood to have their livelihoods eliminated on account of the development of machines that could do their work. This crystallized in the Luddite labor movement of the 19th century that began in Nottingham, England, to oppose the advance of machinery on the basis that it destroyed the livelihoods of textile workers.[38] The origins of Ned Ludd's movement, though, was focused on the impact of technological advance on *employment*. Luddite resistance towards technology was on the basis of job loss, first and foremost.

Today, the term Luddite has a much broader meaning, referring to someone who opposes technology, often implicitly so, on an existential or lifestyle choice basis. Contemporary consternation about the potential for technological advance – now in the form of AI, machine learning, and the platform economy rather than factories full of machines – similarly stems from the worry about the impact of automation on jobs. Forms of technology that replace manual labor and processes are considered to be automation technology. It is defined as a "class of electromechanical equipment that is relatively autonomous once it is set in motion on the basis of predetermined instructions or procedures."[39] This follows from the language of John Maynard Keynes, who in 1930, in his essay on the "economist possibilities of our grandchildren," coined the phrase "technological unemployment," effectively meaning that workers lose their jobs as they are replaced with machines. The different concepts refer to the same core issue: the fact that technologies – once established – do not need (much, if any) human oversight or intervention.

The risk, then, is that jobs are destroyed rather than upgraded on account of technological automation. It is distinct than Schumacher's notion of appropriate technologies, in which technological innovation should support local, existing labor, by making it more productive, rather than replacing it. Technological unemployment was, in the early 20th century, focused on low-skilled workers. Low-skilled workers experienced unemployment, as their jobs were replaced, just as returns concentrated amongst capital owners and the increased earnings of high-skilled workers due to productivity advances.[40] As Glennie and Gabriel assert, this is the "concept of 'skill-biased technological change,' where new technologies create jobs for the highest-skilled people while others get left behind."[41]

What technologies can bring jobs?

Others argue that technological advance is the (long-term) solution to a more equal society, particularly better employment opportunities. Heater posits that "technology is killing jobs, and only technology can save them."[42] He explains that previous epochs of technological advance "didn't lead to mass unemployment as much as a transformation of the work being done."[43] That transformation can be positive, especially in the medium-longer term when reskilling can be completed by those whose jobs are lost. In a similar vein, Bob Doyle of the Association for Advancing Automation asserts that technological advance means that society's "dull, dirty or dangerous jobs"[44] are the ones eradicated, and so upskilling (or reskilling) should be embraced, rather than trying to preserve existing jobs and methods. As an example of this approach, the Vietnamese startup Enablecode innovates ways in which marginalized laborers can find work at the technological frontier, by delineating and providing training for tasks such as "mechanical turk." This represents a new type of labor, involved at the forefront of technology.[45]

What's more, economists have (counterintuitively) shown that firms that invest in technological automation are the firms that *increase* jobs overall, rather than reduce head count. The findings show that the economy's more productive firms *both invest more* in automation, and by virtue of this better management, *hire more*: in particular, more high-skilled workers. Less productive firms may not invest in technological automation, but due to their inferior competitive positioning, they flounder in the market, and are therefore unable to offer more jobs. Aghion et al. assert that "automation goes hand in hand with employment growth," and so technological automation "generates productivity gains that are shared by employees, consumers, and firms."[46] Their findings suggest that more technologically-innovative firms are needed for economic growth and societal well-being. They even go a step further and assert that social mobility is crucially enabled by the ability for new innovations – and the entrepreneurs responsible for developing and selling them – to extract economic rents (profits).[47] The point then being that technological innovation should be embraced for its ability to deliver more high-quality jobs, economic growth, and social mobility. This dovetails with Schumpeter's expectation that creative destruction will bring new accumulations of wealth.

Considering the case for technology as a job creator, and displacer, we assert that each technological innovation has a unique impact on the quantity of jobs created and eliminated. Thus, a more nuanced approach is needed in order to harness the potential benefits of technological innovation, while reducing the harm.

Even if technology can bring jobs, a crucial challenge has to do with who is included. Without purposeful intervention so that more, and different, members of society are able to participate in technological innovation, technology-oriented entrepreneurship is not accessible to all equally.[48] Technology-based entrepreneurship is an employment form that is often most available to those in possession of the needed finance, human, and social capital.[49] This tends to be the (upper) middle class, and those with strong social networks, and can either be expats living in the country or returnees educated abroad.[50] In order to democratize access to such forms of high-powered employment, social capital – which enables access to finance capital and is also associated with the possession of necessary human capital – needs to be purposefully accumulated by those lacking essential social networks and experiences.[51] As a result, activity needs to be designed in a "distribution-sensitive" way, so that wider society is able to participate as potentially high-powered entrepreneurs and innovators.[52]

Who is involved in this approach, and how?

Technology-supported inclusive innovation can provide products and services that are more affordable and tailored to a wider set of needs, improved market access, and enhanced opportunities to use innovative approaches and tools that can boost incomes. Inclusive innovation approaches also strive to empower greater participation in the production of technology-based innovation. Enablecode, which trains and designs work streams so that disabled people are able to code, and Vulcan Augmetics, which creates affordable and high-spec prosthetics, are examples.

Academia has contributed to the rising awareness of inclusive innovation, especially the importance of considering the direction of technological innovation across the region. For instance, through participation in a UNIID-SEA program between 2011 and 2014, Hoa Sen (Lotus) University in Ho Chi Minh City created a curriculum to train tomorrow's leaders in inclusive innovation. The university offers Innovation for Inclusive Development (IID) as a subject in its general education. As the university explained,

> the overall objective for the course is to educate students about inclusive development and IID, and to raise awareness of IID among other university stakeholders and the public.

In this sense, the curriculum aims to grow the volume of potential participants in inclusive innovation and the cadre of policymakers who are attuned to designing governance in an inclusive manner. This is part of the efforts to orient the "triple helix" – of university, industry, and government – towards inclusive innovation for development in Southeast Asia.[53]

Civil society may be involved in this approach as relationship brokers, partners, or participants in the design, prototyping, and implementation stages of the innovation process. See, for example, Socialgiver, based in Thailand, a tech-based social enterprise launched in 2015.[54] Socialgiver aggregates spare capacity from the service industry, such as hotels, restaurants, and tourist activities, onto its digital platform with customers purchasing the service with the amount going towards funding community-driven initiatives and charities across the region. Another example is the Samdrup Jongkhar Initiative (SJI), a civil society organization that drives the advance of AT to solve social and environmental challenges, such as waste management. The SJI is detailed in Box 3.5.

Funders and investors have a role to play as potential sources of financial support and as customers for these technology innovators. For example, the Lotus Hub – an impact investment fund operating across Southeast Asia – works with Vietnamese social enterprises to improve their operations management in order to improve their ability to raise follow-on impact investment funding (seed-stage equity funding as well as follow-on funding) anywhere between US$500,000 and US$3 million.[55] Innovation intermediaries such as accelerators and incubators are also critical. They provide a range of advisory and wraparound support services, signpost funding opportunities, and broker connections between firms and key partners, such as investors or researchers.

Box 3.5 The Samdrup Jongkhar Initiative

By Jayshree Patnaik, Research Scholar, Rajendra Mishra School of Engineering Entrepreneurship, Indian Institute of Technology Kharagpur

Bhutan's economic and moral progress is governed by Gross National Happiness (GNH), an index that measures the well-being and collective happiness of the population. The Samdrup Jongkhar Initiative (SJI) at Dewathang, Bhutan, envisages advancing the GNH model of development by putting the knowledge, values, and principles into practice. The initiative was founded under the patronage of the Lhomon Society by its spiritual leader Dzonsar Jamyang Khyentse Rinpoche, a Buddhist master, filmmaker, and writer, in 2010. SJI was registered as a civil society organization in 2012 with the mission to create resilient, self-reliant, flourishing, and environmentally-sensitive communities in Dewathang. The team comprises ten members; three program officers, two farm attendants, two craft trainers, one account officer, one field assistant, and one Program Director, Mr. Cheku Dorji.

SJI primarily works on four areas: organic agriculture, youth engagement, zero waste, and appropriate technology. According to Cheku Dorji, appropriate technology is "any simple technology that is locally adaptable, and affordable, by the communities." The prime aim of SJI involves: imparting training on best agriculture practice, supporting a lead farmer approach, encouraging traditional crops for value addition, preserving local practice and knowledge, building community seed banks, and strengthening organic farming. SJI aims to develop an eco-village where the notion of community resilience, community vitality, leadership, and soft aspects of technology are more action-driven.

I visited SJI in 2018. There were mainly two activities that caught my attention: (i) practice of zero-waste management and (ii) designing AT to instill food security and sufficiency among farmers. The idea of zero-waste management was given by Rinpoche, as he is an environmental activist. Rinpoche initiated the idea in the community in 2012 and the idea was translated into action by the craft trainers of SJI. The idea of developing AT was a collaborative project between SJI and an engineering institution called the Center for Appropriate Technology at Jigme Namgyal Polytechnic to study the potential use of solar energy. The activities are explained in detail here:

1. Zero-Waste Management Approach (Waste Collection to Wealth Generation): waste minimization and management are practiced in Dewathang by minimizing and recycling plastics. SJI aims to reduce waste generated in different religious ceremonies, events,

and festivals. The approach to waste management consists of seg-regating waste, creating crafts from the waste, and providing zero-waste training manuals. The "waste-to-wealth" approach generated livelihood opportunities for many poor women in the communities and altered how waste is handled. I visited the house of a middle-aged woman named Pema, aged 35, in Dewathang in July 2018, who was actively involved in this zero-waste craft activity. She showed me how she weaves baskets and bags from the discarded plastic bottles. She strips these bottles through a cutter and weaves these bottle strips with the help of a loom installed in her house to produce different sized bags and baskets. This recycling of waste has helped her and other women from communities generate revenue for their families. As Pema explained,

> I do not sit idle in the house anymore. I get the orders from different communities to design baskets. This allows earning extra income for my family. It takes me around one or two days to convert this waste into the final product.

2. Implementing appropriate technology for promoting food self-sufficiency: one outcome of local innovation practice is the solar drier, which is considered an appropriate technology by the farmers and SJI. Farmers from Dewathang cultivate mustard, paddy, legumes, chilies, and drying fruits and vegetables in the open is a long-established tradition. However, when dried in the open, the vegetables catch mold and dust. This problem was brought to the notice of SJI by the farmers. SJI collaborated with the farmers and JNP to design a solar drier using local materials and resources. SJI conducted training to impart knowledge to farmers on how to construct a solar drier at their houses. The technical feasibility of the drier was found to be effective in retaining the nutrient value of the crops. I visited Tshering, aged 40, a farmer in Dewathang who has this solar drier installed in his backyard. According to Tshering,

> My solar drier does not depend on electricity. I can save energy. Because of the solar drier, I do not have to depend on getting vegetables across the border. I can grow my vegetables which will also have a long shelf life. Also, I am selling this fresh produce in the markets, and I am self-sufficient now.

Communities are endowed with indigenous skills and ingenuity. Through local innovation practices and the intervention of SJI, the mobilization of indigenous knowledge can be advanced to create opportunities for improved economic and environmental well-being and ensure the communities' self-sufficiency. According to Cheku Dorji,

> "It is important to tap and consider the indigenous knowledge of communities because the community tells us the exact issue where we can intervene and what kind of technology can help them. We try to develop appropriate technology according to the requirements which will improve their socio-economic conditions and cut down the dependence of importing technology from other developed countries."

The development index of Bhutan is measured with GNH. These two examples of local innovation practice show that instilling a sense of self-reliance and self-sufficiency by developing AT can bring empowerment and happiness.

Around the world, **governments and international organizations** work to foster technological advances that strive to address societal and environmental challenges. International organizations help to direct the aim of innovation towards addressing the problems of the most excluded and underserved members of society. For example, Bambuhay – a UNDP Philippines Tawid COVID-19 Innovation Challenge winner – is seeking to address the twin problems of plastic waste and low incomes in the farming community by supporting the farming and development of bamboo.[56] Bambuhay has developed a line of bamboo mugs, toothbrushes, tumblers, straws, and more, bamboo being a biodegradable and reusable alternative to plastic.

Grassroots innovators – bringing their technical expertise to bear on how technological innovation can be more inclusive – complement and work in concert with other organizations. For example, 1516 Green Energy, in Vietnam, provides low-cost systems of wind turbines and solar panels to generate electricity for the poor in remote areas. 1516 Green Energy applies architectural insights to help deliver renewable energy at a low cost to poor households.

Intermediary organizations, such as accelerators, incubators, and science parks, have proliferated in the region. For instance, in Ho Chi Minh City, the city government created a Hi-Tech Agricultural Park in 2008. The Park's aim is to use technology to better serve the city's agricultural needs by "applying high technology on agriculture" to bolster productivity of specific activities (Investment & Trade Promotion Centre: Ho Chi Minh City, 2019). More specifically, the Park's first three projects focused on (1) cultivation and cattle farming, (2) poultry farming, and (3) aquatic production. The Park is supported by infrastructure provided by the local government, financial support from investors, and expertise from foreign partners. Intermediary organizations such as the Hi-Tech Agricultural Park provide technical and operational support for a burgeoning cohort of socially- and environmentally-minded entrepreneurs and innovators across Southeast Asia.

Collectively, there is a case for **large firms** being part of the "what" for developing and deploying (at scale) inclusive innovation. Large technology firms can promote innovation that propels and transforms society. As a contemporary example of a large firm driving innovation that benefits society, in a May 2016 TED Talk, Astro Teller, the head of Google X – which Google's parent company Alphabet describes as a "moonshot factory" – outlines the team's approach to solving big challenges, such as the need for sustainable food and transportation.[57] The "X team" was working on vertical farming as a way of producing (more) food without needing more agricultural land, and a lighter-than-air-buoyant ship. This means that shaping the direction of big (technology) firms' innovation is essential to addressing environmental and societal challenges.

When large firms employ diverse workforces, they also contribute to greater participation in technological innovation. In the COVID-19 context, in fact, large technology firms played a role in advancing more inclusive employment, by allowing their employees to work from home.[58] The key to large firms being a net contributor to inclusive innovation is that their direction – in product and employment strategy – is focused on diversity and inclusion. The profits may or may not be reinvested in ways that benefit local communities, or wider society. Companies domicile in tax-efficient locales operate online, hire few employees and pay little tax; society – in terms of the local taxpayers and potential laborers – has little to gain. Thus, the question becomes the direction, in this case of large firms, and the extent to which they strive for inclusion.

In terms of **startups and SMEs**, as a result of their alignment with technological innovation, they can be perceived as an engine of capitalism; new entrants to a market that will use technology to shake up existing production structures and challenge incumbent firms.

Yet, entrepreneurs are not necessarily high-growth firms, nor technologically-centered, and of course innovation does not only come from tech-centric entrepreneurship. Global Entrepreneurship Monitor (GEM) has distinguished "necessity-driven early-stage entrepreneur" and "opportunity-driven early-stage entrepreneur" since 2001. Then, from 2005, it added a third category (within "opportunity") called "improvement-driven opportunity early-stage entrepreneur" to capture this intermediate type. Necessity-driven entrepreneurs refers to entrepreneurs who do not seek self-employment, but rather, are forced to create their own work given the absence of other employment options. Implicitly, this form of entrepreneurship is the one that is invoked in the context of the informal economy.

At the opposite end of the spectrum, an opportunity-driven entrepreneur is – as it sounds – one who may leave steady, and even high-quality, employment in order to create a business in which they see an opportunity.[59] Novel and opportunity-driven forms of entrepreneurship most closely align with notions of Schumpeterian entrepreneurs; those who drive processes of creative destruction on account of their challenge to the existing industry or means of production. As instigators of creative destruction, these novel, Schumpeterian entrepreneurs are purported to drive productivity advances that underpin economic growth and innovation. But, routine entrepreneurs do not (1) necessarily drive technological innovation or (2) strive for inclusion. The challenge is to bring together the Schumpeter and Schumacher aims: both productivity gains as well as aiming to enable local labor markets and protect against environmental degradation.

To quote an example, Hydro Plant, which operated in Myanmar before the COVID-19 pandemic, was developing cost-effective, solar-powered smart Internet of Things (IoT) farm control systems for food processors, traditional, aquaculture, and hydroponic farms. These were designed to help farmers reduce operation costs, increase operational efficiency, and gain consistent quality outputs. They aimed to support the creation of modern farms that can access and use farm level, weather, and market data to support precision farming. One of Hydro Plant's impact metrics was the number of farmers reached, focused on reaching individuals who were typically less well-served by technology and innovation. It strived to serve a consumer group (small-scale farmers) to help their productivity and environmental impact; in this sense, it channeled both Schumpeter (innovation that drives productivity gains) *and* Schumacher (appropriate technology that supports local labor and the environment).

Strengths and shortcomings

One of the key strengths of this approach is the potential ability of innovators to identify and respond to social and environmental problems in a responsive and iterative way, leveraging existing platform-based innovation models. They can be disruptive, and test and evaluate innovative solutions that governments and other actors can then take to scale, if there is clear evidence of impact.

However, there is a risk of an overreliance on technological solutions for problems that might also require social or systemic responses. As observed by one interviewee,

> The process of inclusive innovation could produce a new product or service, and should be social, but does not necessarily have to be technological. Technology could be a part of the solution, but ... it is more about the purpose than the means.

For us, technology can address societal challenges, but is not the solution in and of itself. An issue associated with this approach relates to the role that may be played by the beneficiaries of the ideas, products, or services

Box 3.6 Digital Bangladesh: a govpreneur's quest for inclusive innovation

By Ishtiaque Hussain, a2i Bangladesh

"Why did you get married in the first place? And why did you decide to even have me?" 16-year-old Shayan asked his dad jokingly. But this was a question that he had been thinking about for a while now.

Shayan's dad is Anir Chowdhury, a US tech entrepreneur–turned self-styled Bangladeshi "govpreneur," currently serving as the policy advisor for the Bangladesh government's public sector innovation program, a2i.

Born and raised in Bangladesh, Anir went to college in the US initially intending to study physics (mostly because his father, whom he idolized, was a physicist) and then to embark on a life in academia. But he soon realized that he preferred the collective, social nature of problem-solving in applied computer science to the more solitary life of a physicist. After graduating, he founded several tech startups (which were not as "hot" back then as they are now), boasting Fortune 500 companies among their clientele.

Anir now lives and works in Dhaka, the capital of Bangladesh, while Shayan and his mother live in New York. Shayan's question stems from the fact that since Anir started a2i in 2009 (while visiting Bangladesh to do volunteer work around building the capacity of the local IT industry), he has developed a pattern of visiting his family for only a couple of weeks, twice, or three times a year. What's more, he makes the audacious attempt to keep New York hours in Dhaka (a ten-hour difference) to help his son out with his studies while doing what is so much more than just a full-time job to him – a2i, his passion, his calling in life.

What is this a2i that motivates Anir to make such an incredible personal sacrifice? a2i started life as a UNDP-designed eGovernance project housed within and implemented by the Prime Minister's Office as its flagship Digital Bangladesh initiative. It is poised to be formally established as the country's national public sector innovation agency.

But what does a2i actually do and how does it champion inclusive innovation? To understand that, we must first understand whom a2i works for and the context it works in.

Picture dark grey clouds, pouring rain on a tiny, mud-walled hut in a remote, lush green village. It's the middle of July and the monsoon season is upon Bangladesh. Peek through the solitary window and you see a young mother, Ferdowsy, still in her teens, sitting on a jaajim[1] upon the floor. Ferdowsy is staring blankly at the ceiling. As her two-month-old daughter sleeps peacefully on her lap, her own mind is restless, her brain pounding. She is struggling to decide whether she should resume working as a domestic helper. It pays a paltry thousand takas a month (approximately US$13) and she desperately needs the money. But what about her baby?

Ferdowsy's husband Rofik, who pulled rickshaw vans for a living, was killed in a road accident less than a month before the birth of their daughter. The only support she has is the hut they live in which belongs to Rofik's parents, who are poor sharecroppers, both in their late sixties. Together, they are part of the 3.3 million Bangladeshis living in extreme poverty.

Although she doesn't know it, Ferdowsy is eligible for maternity allowance (US$5.89 per month) that is provided by the government as part of its social safety net. However, even if she had known, in order to receive this allowance, first she would need to travel nearly 20 km to the subdistrict nirbahi's (government executive) office just to collect the application form. And this is only half the story. Over the next few visits, she would have to wait for hours in queues, unsure of what the next step was or whom to talk to for getting information, making her an obvious target for unscrupulous middlemen. By the time she would finally complete the application process, Ferdowsy would have had to visit the subdistrict office several times, spanning at least a month and she would spend almost 50 percent of her monthly wage in conveyance fares alone.

This is what the archaic, paper-based public service delivery system expects of a woman applying for maternity allowance. Let alone one who also happens to be a poor widow. In most cases, access to government services starts with citizens having to collect an application form, complete, and submit it along with related documents, photographs of the applicant, and necessary fees. Sounds simple enough. Right?

What does Ferdowsy think? Would it be easy or even make sense for her to leave her two-month-old daughter at home and travel 40 km up and down from the subdistrict government office just to collect a form? No. The mind boggles when one considers how the baby would fare if she opted to take her along.

Next, would Ferdowsy be able to fill up the application? Unclear. She was an eighth-grade dropout, it is unlikely that her application would be flawless.

Where would she get photographed? Not at the office where she got the application form. At the very least, would she be able to pay the necessary fees there? No, that would only be possible at a state-owned bank that was located elsewhere.

Ferdowsy's challenge in accessing public services was precisely the kind of unsexy, unpopular, far from "cutting-edge" but very real problem that Anir attempted to take on through a2i.

He assembled a team composed of outstanding civil servants hand-picked from different levels of bureaucracy – from the field level all the way up to senior bureaucrats based in the capital – as well as private sector experts (change management, design thinking, IT, mobile money, etc.) and people with experience working with NGOs, academics, and student volunteers.

Together, they created space for experimentation within the public sector in Bangladesh and used insights derived from that experience to design an ecosystem for digital service access that promoted inclusion rather than widening the digital divide.

They developed an "empathy training" course that arranges for relatively senior government officers to act as secret shoppers and visit citizens' access points for services outside of their ministry or area of expertise. Doctors are sent to schools, teachers to land offices, and land officers to hospitals. Without administrative knowledge or official privileges, officers find themselves in citizens' shoes as mere customers. This experience helps participants develop a critical eye that they use to scrutinize their own agency's delivery systems and simplify them by dropping unnecessary steps, prior to digitization. Upon completion of this training, civil servants can also apply for funding to experiment with ideas. The best ideas receive scale-up funding and they are also taken nationally.

They also launched the Bangladesh National Portal which was designed to bring over 42,000 government offices and literally thousands of application forms to the myriad citizen-facing services onto one single web address: www.bangladesh.gov.bd. This made the application forms, like the one Ferdowsy would have had to fill in, available anywhere, anytime, at the click of a button.

But, of course, Ferdowsy is not expected to go online and fill in a digital application form. That was where the Digital Centres – one of the innovations that received scale-up funding – came in. The idea was that people like Ferdowsy would describe what they wanted and the Digital Centre entrepreneurs would look into the National Portal, find the right application forms, fill it in, and submit on behalf of the applicants. Since all the 6,500+ centers (one for every eight to ten villages) were also equipped with digital cameras and functioned as mobile money agents, she would not only be able to get photographed and complete the application process by paying any fees necessary, she would also be able to collect her allowance from the same center as well.

And the same was true for hundreds of other services. The National Portal also featured service profile books on all the 600 e-services that it hosted. The books contained service profiles and process maps. Each profile included information starting from the name of the service provider and average time required for service delivery all the way to contact details of relevant officials for grievance redressal, i.e., in cases of service delivery failure. The process maps offered visual aids to walk them through the steps of accessing a service. Each step of the service delivery procedure was portrayed in a visual format.

The resulting unprecedented, citizen-centered transformation of public services has saved Bangladeshi citizens nearly US$8 billion[2] over the span of the last decade, in terms of TCV[3] reduction alone. For example, in the 131 years between 1873 and 2004, only 8 percent of the Bangladeshi population were registered. Contrast that to the picture painted in ten years between 2009 and 2018: nearly 130 million citizens out of 160 million, an 80 percent coverage, was achieved. The average time to register births went down from over ten days to below five hours, a 98 percent reduction, the average cost went down by 40 percent, and the number of visits to complete a birth registration was reduced by 40 percent.

These tremendous results can be squarely attributed to the availability of an electronic birth registration system (digitization) that was decentralized to the Digital Centres (inclusive means to access services) and crucially, a "nudge" (empathy-driven, citizen-centric innovation) in the form of making birth certificates mandatory for admitting children into primary schools.

In March 2020, COVID-19 reached Bangladesh. With the nation in the grips of its first countrywide lockdown, there were only a couple of RT-PCR[60] labs and a short supply of testing kits. The national information hotline (accessible through and popularly known by its dial in short code "333") that the a2i team had initially designed as a means for primarily illiterate citizens to seek information about government services and grievance redress was repurposed as a helpline to enable millions of people without smartphones (two-thirds of the Bangladeshi population) to self-report symptoms of the virus.

In an organic way, 333 evolved into a telemedicine line that enabled over half a million COVID-19 patients and 2.4 million pregnant women to receive medical advice. Moreover, the platform was revised several times, including as an emergency response to curb child marriage and to provide food support to families facing food insecurity during lockdowns.

a2i's 333 also formed the basis for a national, collective data intelligence system that enabled the secure sharing of anonymized data between telecommunications companies and the government to launch syndromic surveillance in order to track disease progression seven to ten days before COVID-19 testing, helping save lives.

Almost equally important to Anir, a2i also helped him realize that the government innovation system was more inclusive than he could ever imagine. As he discovered through his serendipitous foray into public service, there is a major opportunity for ordinary citizens from different walks of life to play a more active role in creating the conditions for a different type of innovation altogether.

Anir's way of articulating it is,

> The world needs more "Govpreneurs." People who work like private sector entrepreneurs, not just with, but from within, the government, replacing the profit motive with the pursuit of enhancing public value. Individuals who through their creativity, strategy, networking, negotiation and persuasion are able to bring new ideas into government and promote more inclusive innovation policies that are more focused on the nature of the complex challenges we face today rather than single point solutions.

To Anir, the philosophy underpinning Digital Bangladesh embodies this spirit of inclusive innovation. Digital Bangladesh immediately makes one think of a futuristic Bangladesh, one that has 5G internet, 100 percent smartphone penetration, smart homes with smart appliances, AI and robots doing all sorts of household tasks. The Internet of Things (IoT).

Safe to say, that would be the elitist perception of most people who are already economically privileged and educated enough to be aware of the things listed above in the first place.

> What is often forgotten is that the majority of people right around the world do not belong to the privileged class. Take the average Bangladeshi – for example, living in a second or third tier town, subdistrict or village – they are not thinking about AI, or 5G internet, or robots, and are frankly not close to being ready for them either, be it due to cost, accessibility, or even skill. Those Bangladeshis are just trying to make their lives a bit better, are trying to get closer to the "digital" lives that their richer, more educated, urban counterparts are living.

That's how Anir articulates the true purpose of Digital Bangladesh.

As such, the primary mission of Digital Bangladesh is not to improve the internet, or to facilitate e-commerce platforms, or to usher in robots and AI. Rather, it is about designing digital solutions that would help citizens like Ferdowsy, those without internet, those without smartphones, and help bridge that "digital divide" that inhibits even the accessing of public services – one which undoubtedly exists and threatens to widen as a result of the pandemic.

Individuals like Anir who have had the opportunity to serve as Govpreneurs acquire tacit knowledge about how to get things done in government. This knowledge is often difficult to share because the knowledge, skills, and heuristics they acquire are often dependent on the particular context they are operating in. Thus, Anir agreed to an interview for writing this story in part because he feels the best way to scale inclusive innovation is for the innovators to share what they have learned through storytelling or, "reflecting out loud" as he calls it. And in part, it is his way of attempting to entice the reader to consider public service at some point in their career.

Ending where we started, with Shayan. Right after graduating high-school in the fall of 2019, he came to visit his dad for the first time in Dhaka, planning to spend a month. Around the same time, COVID-19 hit and that one month turned into a whole year. Just Shayan and his dad spending more time than they had ever spent together, quality time, "locked down" in an apartment in Dhaka.

And during this time, Shayan got to see up close his dad in action and the impact that his work was creating. One day, over dinner, Shayan quietly said, "Dad, I understand now."

[1] Bengali for a thin mattress stuffed with cotton that is used as a makeshift bed.
[2] To date, according to calculations by the Bangladesh Bureau of Statistics.
[3] A byword for innovation in the Bangladesh Civil Service: innovation equals something that reduces for citizens the "Time" (T) to receive a service from application to final delivery; "cost" (C) to receive a service including all cost components including real and opportunity costs from application to final delivery; and number of "visits" (V) to various government offices from application to final delivery.

developed by technology-oriented startups. Founders of these organizations typically have a personal or professional connection to the challenges they are trying to solve, but are not necessarily problem-owners themselves. This potentially creates a situation where they may innovate *for* underserved communities rather than *with* them, and in doing so, unwittingly reinforce existing inequalities in terms of access to power and opportunities.

Notes

1 UNCTAD, "The need for an honest discussion on technology and development." May 13, 2019. https://unctad.org/news/need-honest-discussion-technology-and-development.

2 Aghion, Antonin, and Bunel, *The Power of Creative Destruction*, 176.

3 The Economist, "Race and sex bias in medicine: how medicine discriminates against non-white people and women." April 10, 2021.

4 For more on the cognitive and social benefits of diversity in technological innovation, see Michael Li, "To build less-biased AI, hire a more-diverse team." *Harvard Business Review.* October 26, 2020. https://hbr.org/2020/10/to-build-less-biased-ai-hire-a-more-diverse-team. Xiao-Hua (Frank) Wang, Tae-Yeol Kim, and Deog-Ro Lee, "Cognitive diversity and team creativity: effects of team intrinsic motivation and transformational leadership." *Journal of Business Research* 69, no. 9 (2016): 3231–3239.

5 Paul Mozur, "A genocide incited on Facebook, with posts from Myanmar's military." *The New York Times.* October 15, 2018. www.nytimes.com/2018/10/15/technology/myanmar-facebook-genocide.html. We thank Giulio Quaggiotto for making this point in his review of a draft of the manuscript.

6 Nesta's (2018) inclusive innovation framework.

7 Jacques Bughin, Eric Hazan, Tera Allas, Klemens Hjartar, James Manyika, Pal Erik Sjatil, and Irina Shigina, "'Tech for good': using technology to smooth disruption and improve well-being." *McKinsey Global Institute.* May 15, 2019. www.mckinsey.com/featured-insights/future-of-work/tech-for-good-using-technology-to-smooth-disruption-and-improve-well-being.

8 Richard Culatta, *Digital for Good: Raising Kids to Thrive in an Online World* (Cambridge, MA: Harvard Business Review Press, 2021).

9 World Bank, *Solar Program Brings Electricity to Off-the-Grid Rural Areas in Bangladesh.* October 10, 2016. www.worldbank.org/en/news/feature/2016/10/10/solar-program-brings-electricity-off-grid-rural-areas.

10 Investment and Trade Promotion Centre: Ho Chi Minh City, "Hi-tech agricultural park: information on hi-tech agricultural park, functional and expansion zones etc." November 11, 2021. www.itpc.gov.vn/web/en.

11 Zon Pann Pwint, "Silicon Valley technology comes to Myanmar." *Myanmar Times.* March 13, 2020. www.mmtimes.com/news/silicon-valley-technology-comes-myanmar.html.

12 Time, "Best inventions of 2001: food cooling system." October 11, 2021. http://content.time.com/time/specials/packages/article/0,28804,1936165_1936254_1936632,00.html.

13 Gernot Brodnig, Elaine Chee, Ashutosh Raina, Zoe True, and Aly Rahim, "Inclusive disruption: harnessing the social power of technology." *World Bank Blog.* March 26, 2020. https://blogs.worldbank.org/governance/inclusive-disruption-harnessing-social-power-technology.

14 *The Economist*, "India's high-tech governance risks leaving behind its poorest citizens." October 16, 2021. www.economist.com/asia/2021/10/16/indias-high-tech-governance-risks-leaving-behind-its-poorest-citizens.

15 WHO, *Blindness and Vision Impairment.* October 14, 2021. www.who.int/news-room/fact-sheets/detail/blindness-and-visual-impairment.

16 Sandy Phan, "3D printers: significance in alleviating poverty." *Borgen Magazine*. January 28, 2015. www.borgenmagazine.com/3d-printers-significance-alleviating-poverty/.

17 Alexandru Pîrjan and Dana-Mihaela Petroşanu, "The impact of 3D printing technology on the society and economy." *Journal of Information Systems and Operations Management* 7, no. 2 (2013): 360–370.

18 Alan Foley and Beth A. Ferri, "Technology for people, not disabilities: ensuring access and inclusion." *Journal of Research in Special Educational Needs* 12, no. 4 (2012): 192–200.

19 Gregg C. Vanderheiden, "Ubiquitous accessibility, common technology core, and micro assistive technology: commentary on 'Computers and people with disabilities.'" *ACM Transactions on Accessible Computing* 1, no. 2 (2008): 10:1–10:7.

20 Nicola Crosta and Allison Sanders, *Social Enterprises and Disability: Fostering Innovation, Awareness and Social Impact in the ASEAN Region* (Economic Research Institute for ASEAN and East Asia, September 2021).

21 Majid Ezzati and Daniel M. Kammen, "The health impacts of exposure to indoor air pollution from solid fuels in developing countries: knowledge, gaps, and data needs." *Environmental Health Perspectives* 110, no. 11 (2002): 1057–1068.

22 UNCTAD, *Renewable Energy Technologies for Rural Development: Current Studies on Science, Technology and Innovation*. April 2010. https://unctad.org/system/files/official-document/dtlstict20094_en.pdf.

23 Alex Rau, Rob Toker, and Joanne Howard, "Can technology really save us from climate change?" *Harvard Business Review*. January–February 2010. https://hbr.org/2010/01/can-technology-really-save-us-from-climate-change.

24 Mike DiCicco, "NASA technologies spin off to fight climate change." *NASA Global Climate Change Blog*. April 21, 2021. https://climate.nasa.gov/blog/3075/nasa-technologies-spin-off-to-fight-climate-change/.

25 Farhad Fathieh, Markus J. Kalmutski, Eugene A. Kapustin, Peter J. Waller, Jingjing Yang, and Omar M. Yaghi, "Practical water production from desert air." *Science Advances* 4, no. 6 (2018).

26 World Bank, "Trends in solid waste management." October 11, 2021. https://datatopics.worldbank.org/what-a-waste/trends_in_solid_waste_management.html.

27 Catherine Clifford, "Trillions of pounds of trash: new technology tries to solve an old garbage problem." *CNBC*. May 29, 2021. www.cnbc.com/2021/05/29/can-new-technology-solve-a-trillion-pound-garbage-problem.html.

28 Avantium, "FDCA and plantMEG™ together make a 100% plant-based plastic PEF." October 11, 2021. www.avantium.com/lead-products/#pef&fdca/.

29 Schumacher, *Small Is Beautiful*.

30 Pursell, "The rise and fall of the appropriate technology movement," 631.

31 See Jequier, *Appropriate Technology;* Dickson, *Alternative Technology.*

32 Pursell, "The rise and fall of the appropriate technology movement," 632.

33 Kaplinsky, "Schumacher meets Schumpeter."

34 Pursell, "The rise and fall of the appropriate technology movement," 631.

35 Kaplinsky, "Schumacher meets Schumpeter."

36 Poh Kam Wong, Yuen Ping Ho, and Erkko Autio, "Entrepreneurship, innovation and economics growth." *Small Business Economics* 24 (2005): 336.

37 *The Economist*, "The Tories are deadline serious about levelling up." October 9, 2021. www.economist.com/news/the-tories-are-deadly-serious-about-levelling-up/21805357.

38 Kevin Hjortshøj O'Rourke, Ahmed S Rahman, and Alan M. Taylor, "Luddites, the industrial revolution, and the demographic transition." *Journal of Economic Growth* 18 (2013): 373–409.

39 Aghion, Antonin, and Bunel, *The Power of Creative Destruction,* 51.

40 Aghion, Antonin, and Bunel, *The Power of Creative Destruction,* 50.

41 Alex Glennie and Madeleine Gabriel, "Is there a role for innovation in tackling global inequality?" *Nesta.* September 11, 2017. www.nesta.org.uk/blog/is-there-a-role-for-innovation-in-tackling-global-inequality/.

42 Brian Heater, "Technology is killing jobs, and only technology can save them." *TechCrunch.* March 26, 2017. https://techcrunch.com/2017/03/26/technology-is-killing-jobs-and-only-technology-can-save-them/.

43 Heater, "Technology is killing jobs."

44 As cited in Heater, "Technology is killing jobs."

45 Mechanical turk – the performance of discrete tasks that computers are able to do, or accurately validate – is not without its critics. Semuels (2018) explains that these new types of jobs are poorly paid, repetitive, and precarious in that workers need to be readily available for tasks or gigs without employment packages and the associated benefits. Alana Semuels, "The internet is enabling a new kind of poorly paid hell." *The Atlantic.* January 23, 2018. www.theatlantic.com/business/archive/2018/01/amazon-mechanical-turk/551192/.

46 Aghion, Antonin, and Bunel, *The Power of Creative Destruction.* Also, we note that the jobs lost, due to automation, are not necessarily reformulated into jobs for similar workers.

47 Aghion, Antonin, and Bunel, *The Power of Creative Destruction,* 81.

48 Hans Westlund and Roger Bolton, "Local social capital and entrepreneurship." *Small Business Economics* 21, no. 2 (2003): 77–113; Lazonick and Mazzucato, "The risk-reward nexus in the innovation-inequality relationship."

49 Steven Samford and Dan Breznitz, "Mending the net: public strategies for the remediation of network failures." *Social Forces.* April 19, 2021. https://doi.org/10.1093/sf/soab031.

50 Paula Mejia and Marcela Melendez, "Middle-class entrepreneurs and social mobility through entrepreneurship in Colombia." *Inter-American Development Bank* working paper no. IDB-WP-317. September 2012; Robyn Klingler-Vidra, Berlin Tran, and Adam Chalmers, "Transnational experience and high-performing entrepreneurs in emerging economies: evidence from Vietnam." *Technology in Society* 66 (2021). DOI: 10.1016/j.techsoc.2021.101605.

51 Klingler-Vidra and Liu, "Inclusive innovation policy as social capital accumulation strategy."

52 Zehavi and Breznitz, "Distribution-sensitive innovation policies."

53 Boon Kwee Ng, Thiruchelvam Kanagasundram, Chan-Yuan Wong, and V.G.R. Chandran, "Innovation for inclusive development in Southeast Asia: the roles of regional coordination mechanisms." *The Pacific Review* 29, no. 4 (2016): 573–602.

54 See https://ecosystem.startupthailand.org/startup/social-giver for more information on Socialgiver.

55 For more information on Lotus Hub, see www.lotusimpact.com/lotushub.

56 Klingler-Vidra and Lor, "Bringing the environment back into our understanding of inclusive innovation."

57 Astro Teller, the head of Google X, May 2016 TED Talk on "The unexpected benefit of celebrating failure." www.youtube.com/watch?v=2t13Rq4oc7A.

58 *The Economist*, "The rise of working from home." April 11, 2021. www.economist. com/special-report/2021/04/08/the-rise-of-working-from-home.
59 Acs et al. (2016) distinguishes types of entrepreneurs in a related way, speaking in terms of "novel" and "routine" entrepreneurship. Routine entrepreneurs are creating a new firm, a new entrant to the market, but are not developing a novel product or process. Novel entrepreneurship, in contrast, involves innovation in the product or the process in which the business is operating. Zoltan J. Acs, Thomas Åstebro, David B. Audretsch, and David T. Robinson, "Public policy to promote entrepreneurship: a call to arms." *Small Business Economics* 47, no. 1 (2016): 35–51.
60 RT-PCR refers to "Reverse transcription-polymerase chain reaction," which is a laboratory technique.

4 Where

Innovation everywhere

The "where" approach to inclusive innovation has to do with reducing spatial determinism by treating innovation as an economic process, designed to strengthen existing systems and better distribute the production of innovation. Efforts relating to the approach that we have termed "innovation everywhere" focus on boosting the innovation capabilities and volumes of areas that – if left alone – would not automatically become innovation-active locations.

In this chapter, we look at why and how innovation activities, and the benefits they produce, have historically become concentrated in specific regions and areas, and the impact this has on economic and social development. We consider the COVID-19 pandemic as a "critical juncture," potentially offering opportunities to drive innovation within communities that are located outside of traditional innovation centers, or that are distributed physically but connected virtually. Drawing on case studies and stories, we explore government-led policies as well as initiatives driven by different actors that strive to achieve a better spatial distribution of innovation activities – expanding beyond capital cities and traditional innovation clusters, to rural and mountainous areas, and to disadvantaged socioeconomic areas. Finally, we consider some of the strengths and shortcomings of this approach, and identify a number of critical questions that it raises (Table 4.1).

We start with the Philippines and its geography as an example of the importance of spatial inclusion in the context of innovation. As an archipelago of more than 7,500 islands, economic activity – and opportunity – is unevenly distributed. Rates of poverty in rural areas are much higher than in urban areas, and over the past few decades, successive Filipino governments have attempted to use science, technology, and innovation policies to drive a process of local development and economic growth.[1] In 2017, this culminated in the launch of an Inclusive Innovation Industrial Strategy, which put the issue of regional economic imbalances front and center. Rafaelita Aldaba, Undersecretary for the Competitiveness and Innovation Group of the Philippine Department of Trade and Industry (DTI), and a key architect of this policy, told us in 2019 that the Inclusive Innovation Industrial Strategy had been developed:

DOI: 10.4324/9781003125877-4

Table 4.1 Where: key concepts and sections

Key concepts	Agglomeration; clusters; critical juncture; exclusion; industrial districts; Marshallian Trinity; migration; NIS; spatial; urban/rural
Sections	Where: the role of place in innovation.
	Where does innovation happen across Southeast Asia?
	Where is exclusion happening?
	Where do policies strive for spatially inclusive innovation?
	Where has COVID-19 acted as a critical juncture?
	Who is involved in this approach, and how?
	Strengths and shortcomings.

> To ensure that our innovation programs reach the greatest number of people and as many areas as possible, in order to address poverty and inequality.

Since then, a network of eight Regional Inclusive Innovation Centers have been established across the Philippines – spaces that bring together innovation agents who collaborate to commercialize market-oriented research and drive competitiveness and entrepreneurship across the country's regions.

Southeast Asia is not alone in this challenge. Research has found that where people live plays a determining role in their access to economic opportunities, and in turn, to their likelihood of being involved in or benefiting from innovation. In their study of social mobility, Chetty et al. found that one's hometown can have a significant impact on lifetime economic prospects.[2] Related research has shown that children growing up in innovation clusters – areas with large universities, research centers, and with a high concentration of businesses – are more likely to be inventors themselves, likely because of the early exposure that they have to innovative ideas and people. It has been suggested that there are many "lost Einsteins" as a result: a large cohort of potential innovators who would have developed impactful inventions if they had been exposed to innovation in their early years. The effect is expected to be especially pronounced among women, nonbinary and gender nonconforming people, ethnic minorities, and children from low-income families.[3]

Where: the role of place in innovation

To link theory to practice, we start by exploring why innovation is said to occur – and advance – in spatial clusters. In *Principles of Economics*, Marshall established the idea of industrial districts, which are areas with a concentration of firms operating in similar product lines.[4] His idea of industrial districts has come to comprise the "Marshallian Trinity": shared workforce, shared inputs/outputs, shared knowledge. For Marshall, location in an industrial district promised (1) hereditary skill, (2) the growth of subsidiary trades, (3) the use of highly specialized machinery, (4) a local market for special skill,

(5) industrial leadership, and (6) the introduction of novelties.[5] Industrial districts, then, possess competitive advantages on account of the specific physical capital (e.g. machinery), human capital, and development of pertinent consumer markets.

A related concept used in academic literature on the spatial clustering of industrial activity (and economic activity) is that of "agglomeration." Agglomeration means the external economies of scale, which deliver benefits of co-location of people and firms in order to reduce costs and advance productivity. Physical co-location stands to benefit industrial capacity on account of decreased transport costs, robust goods supply channels, information sharing, infrastructure and service providers, and the supply of talent and trained workers.[6]

Theory and work on "clusters" is also relevant here as a contemporary application of Marshallian districts. Michael Porter, in his seminal work on the topic, defines clusters as follows:

> Geographic concentrations of interconnected companies and institutions in a particular field. Clusters encompass an array of linked industries and other entities important to competition… A cluster allows each member to benefit *as if* it had a greater scale or *as if* it had joined with others without sacrificing its flexibility.[7]

The geographical proximity of these institutions allows ideas to circulate and grow more quickly than they would otherwise.

More recently, and in a nod to Marshall's industrial districts, the idea of "innovation districts" has emerged – defined broadly as geographic areas where leading-edge "anchor" institutions (such as research universities or research-oriented medical hospitals) and companies cluster and connect with startups, business incubators, and accelerators.[8] Innovation districts have been described as an evolution of the traditional science park model – that of campus settings that are often located in hard-to-reach areas – given their integration into urban systems and infrastructure. Although they take a variety of forms, common characteristics include being physically compact, easily accessible, designed for high levels of digital connectivity, and situated alongside mixed-use housing, office, and retail spaces.[9]

With changes in the contemporary mode of capitalism and technological advance, the benefits of co-location are no longer (entirely) about "being anchored on big physical assets."[10] Jerome Engel's work on global clusters of innovation in the 21st century focuses on assessing "hard factors" (universities, government, entrepreneurs, venture capital, mature corporations, research centers, and service providers) and "soft factors" (mobility of resources, entrepreneurial processes, global strategic perspective, alignment of interests, and global connections).[11]

The hard factors, however, are less about physical infrastructure, and instead, about tangible and intangible assets. The contemporary equivalent of physical assets relates to organizations and the location of ecosystem players, rather than either machinery or transportation costs. Similarly, the soft factors, or the human and social capital endowments, have more to do with mobility and knowledge diffusion on a wider geographic basis. Thus, from a built environment perspective, the scale of clusters – especially the intangibles, or soft factors – reaches well beyond the specific geographic location.

Other work that strives to unpack why innovation clusters occur includes the *Geography of Genius*, in which Eric Weiner explores historical cases of the most creative clusters, in spatial and temporal terms, in order to distil the commonalities of places that were exceptionally creative – or innovative.[12] This includes ancient Athens, Edinburgh during the Enlightenment, Florence during the Renaissance, and Silicon Valley in the 21st century. While they were all different in the particular type of genius they exhibited, Weiner argues, they share characteristics with respect to society's organization, composition, and tastes.

He identifies three core ingredients, which he calls the "3Ds" of outperformance: (1) disorder, (2) diversity, and (3) discernment. Rather than hard factors, and logistical concerns such as shared machinery and transportation proximity, as in industrial districts or in agglomeration theory, Weiner focuses more on cultural determinants. Disorder – which can come on account of war, political upheaval, or other forces – leads to a society that embraces ambiguity and uncertainty, and is thus less locked into predefined, or existing, paths. It is more open to new ideas, and thus, more likely to be creative. Disorder, Weiner asserts, is "necessary to shake up the status quo."[13] Diversity, for its part, refers to the presence of different vantage points together in one place. This can be the result of trade routes, as in ancient Athens or Florence. The point being that transnational experience, and migration, as well as other notions of diversity lend to a creative environment. Finally, discernment, by which Weiner means what a society values, or what they choose to keep, matters. If society values art, as in Renaissance Florence, then innovations occur in art; if it values technology entrepreneurship, as in Silicon Valley, then energy and talent come together in creative ways in that area.

Weiner's work comes from a very different field, but aligns with literature on national innovation systems (NIS).[14] NIS refers to the institutional components that shape the innovation capacity and outputs of a place, in terms of firms, universities, the public sector, finance, and more. Studies delineate distinct components of the system, and work to ascertain which elements determine the nature and performance of the national system. Taking the scale to a more local level, regional systems of innovation (RSI), particularly in cities and major urban areas, explore similar elements, but within these more focused geographies.

Using Silicon Valley as an exemplar of the conditions required for innovation excellence, Adams points to certain factors as the source of Silicon Valley's success: the availability of financial and legal resources, low-risk capital from federal-provided funding, and located in the world's richest country and hence the access to key sources, including the agriculture, extractive, and transportation industries.[15] Adams further suggests that Silicon Valley's success is due to the entrepreneurial system being a result of "being at the right place at the right time," thus pointing at endogenous factors that support the creation of opportunities for innovation in certain areas and not others.

Providing a similar analysis in China, Xu et al. study Chinese provinces, challenging the assumption that innovation will necessarily lead to economic growth.[16] The authors describe the unequal economic growth that is witnessed in Chinese provinces, pointing to negative impacts of innovation in certain areas and positive impacts in others. The authors highlight internal factors for the lack of growth in some areas, namely human capital and its impact on growth potential, trade openness as a positive influence, and institutional corruption as a hindrance to growth.

Scholarship has pointed to different scales, and types, of locales as drivers of Schumpeterian processes of creative destruction over time. In Marshallian terms, the industrial district could be in a city, or on the outskirts. But then, suburbanization (of residential and then industry) in the 20th century decimated urban life. Companies, and their technological capabilities, moved to industrial and science parks in suburban settings, creating large purpose-built campuses, enjoying relatively less expensive real estate, and aligning with the larger societal move out of cities.

This trend reversed in the 21st century, with the "convergence of technology, lifestyle trends, and cultural preferences" leading to "spontaneous emergence of clusters of innovation in cities" – in select cities – the innovation districts described previously.[17]

> Cities, especially large cities, are where it all happens in terms of economic development and innovation, knowledge generation and diffusion, the availability of skilled personnel, important transport nodes and the housing of both people and firms.[18]

Thus, cities have grown as centers of innovation since the 1990s, on account of their bringing together diverse people in terms of skills, backgrounds, etc. However, not all cities are innovative power houses, and not all are innovative in the same way.

Before considering the impact of this concentration of innovative activity in particular places and regions, we pause to look at the geography of innovation in Southeast Asia, highlighting key features of the innovation and development paths taken by different countries, and exploring the way in which inclusive innovation has been conceptualized with reference to the region.

Where does innovation happen across Southeast Asia?

The industrialization of Southeast Asia over recent decades has been driven largely by demand for exports and by high levels of foreign direct investment.[19]

Many countries in the region have been integrated into global value chains, facilitated in part by China's exponential economic growth since the late 1970s, and the subsequent increase of investment flows, cross-border flows, and bilateral trade across the wider region. By leveraging international and regional demand, the region's markets have expanded, the costs of trading have been lowered, and the amount of investment capital has increased.[20]

Rapid urbanization has also transformed the pace and nature of economic growth and development across Southeast Asia, although unevenly and with varied consequences. Of its 11 countries, Singapore is the most developed economy and is considered to be fully urbanized. Malaysia and Brunei are also highly urbanized (with rates of more than 75 percent), while the majority of the rest – Indonesia, Thailand, the Philippines, Laos, Myanmar, and Vietnam – are classified as semiurbanized (with rates of 30–60 percent). Cambodia is still considered to be mostly rural.

Urbanization is usually considered to be a driver of economic growth and rising living standards, although as Florida observes, some countries may be facing a risk of urbanization without growth.[21] As a McKinsey and Company report asserts, cities across Southeast Asia are struggling to cope with the demands for infrastructure and services that accompany a rapid pace of urban growth, including decent housing, water, electricity, transit, healthcare, and education.[22] At the same time, many fast-growing cities in this region are a "blank canvas where infrastructure can spread, unhindered by outdated technology."[23]

While agriculture, manufacturing, and natural resource exports have traditionally been key economic activities for emerging economies, the digital transformation taking place over the past decade has shifted the geography of economic activity and innovation across the region.[24] Southeast Asian countries are witnessing changes in connection with the advance of the digital economy. Illustrating this trend, the Global Innovation Index 2020 identified Thailand as the number one country in business R&D globally, while Malaysia ranks at the world frontier in terms of high-tech net exports.[25]

A number of different innovation paths can be observed across this heterogeneous region. At one end is Singapore, an advanced "frontier" economy with leading scores on many global innovation indicators, and extremely high GDP per capita. At the other end are countries such as Cambodia, Laos, and Myanmar, which require significant investment in infrastructure and governance structures to build their innovation capabilities. In the middle are a group of "catch up" and "learning" countries, for whom a focus on science and technology or innovation-led growth is relatively recent but growing in importance as an underpinning of economic development strategies.[26] Table 4.2 illustrates the development stages of Southeast Asian countries, and the necessary policies required to correspond with the innovation phase they are in.

A 2020 study of innovation in Southeast Asia noted the importance of pro-innovation government policies and investment in science and technology in driving innovation.[27] Moreover, many academic institutions and startups

Table 4.2 Typology of policy frameworks in ASEAN[71]

Phase	Basic infrastructure	High-tech infrastructure	Network cohesion	Global integration
Initial conditions (1) Cambodia, Laos, Myanmar*	Political stability and efficient basic structure.	Emergence of demand for technology.	Social bonds driven by the spirit to compete and achieve.	Linking with regional and global markets.
Learning (2) Thailand, Philippines, Indonesia, Vietnam	Strengthening of basic infrastructure with better customs and bureaucratic coordination.	Learning by doing and imitation.	Expansion of tacitly occurring social institutions to formal intermediary organizations to stimulate connections and coordination between economic agents.	Access to foreign sources of knowledge, imports of material and capital goods, and Foreign Direct Investment (FDI) inflows. Integration in global value chain.
Catch-up (3) Malaysia	Smooth links between economic agents.	Creative destruction activities start here through imports of machinery and equipment, licensing and creative duplication.	Participation of intermediary and government organizations in coordinating technology inflows, initiation of commercially viable R&D.	Licensing and acquisition of foreign capabilities. Upgrading synergies through technology imports. Emergence of strong technology-based exports.

(*continued*)

Table 4.2 Cont.

Phase	Basic infrastructure	High-tech infrastructure	Network cohesion	Global integration
Advanced (4)	Advanced infrastructure to support the meeting demands of economic agents.	Developmental research to accelerate creative destruction activities. Frequent filing of patents in the USA starts here.	Strong participation of intermediary and government organization in coordinating technology inflows, initiation of commercially viable R&D.	Access to foreign human capital, knowledge linkages, and competitiveness in high-tech products and collaboration with R&D institutions.
Frontier (5) Singapore	Novel infrastructure developed to save resource costs and stimulate short lead times.	Basic research R&D labs to support creative accumulation activities. Generating knowledge. Technology shapers generate invention and design patents extensively here.	Participation of intermediary organization in two-way flows of knowledge between producers and users	Connecting to frontier nodes of knowledge and competitive export of high-tech products.

Source: Authors adapted by Ambashi, "Innovation Policy in/for ASEAN," 221.

are using technology to address social development challenges, which is both disrupting traditional business models while also supporting the uptake of new technologies at an unprecedented pace. But how is the inclusive innovation agenda being thought of, and applied, across the region?

In the past decade, the concept of inclusive innovation has received increased attention from practitioners, academia, and policymakers across the ASEAN region.[28] In 2008, a seminal study was published by the IDRC on "Research Councils and Support Organizations in Southeast Asia: Institutions, Issues and Collaboration." It identified "considerations of equity and poverty reduction, and the need for innovation and for the BoP" as a key issue for the region. The study urged for regional dialogues on:

> connecting innovation support systems, usually quite oriented to the modern sector, to traditional sectors and poorer communities ... particularly with respect to agriculture and resource sectors, and rural infrastructure and services.[29]

Since then, a number of cross-regional and national "inclusive innovation" initiatives designed to address the needs of the most disadvantaged can be identified. Following on from the 2008 report, the IDRC initiated the Innovations for the Base of Pyramid (iBoP Asia) project in partnership with Ateneo de Manila University in the Philippines. The focus was the "development and application of technologies to serve the need[s] of [the] poorest population" across six Southeast Asian countries: the Philippines, Indonesia, Singapore, Cambodia, Thailand, and Vietnam.[30]

In 2011, UNIID-SEA the Universities and Councils Network on IID in Southeast Asia project was launched, which emphasized (1) field-building, (2) paradigm-shifts in higher-education and research, (3) building a community of excellence, and (4) policy contribution at the national and ASEAN levels. In the program prospectus, inclusive innovation for development is defined as:

> innovation that reduces poverty and enables all groups of people, especially the poor and marginalized, to participate in decision-making, create and actualize opportunities, and share the benefits of development.[31]

Southeast Asian countries now face varying innovation-related challenges in their economic growth and inclusive innovation paths. It remains to be seen what impacts COVID-19 will have on the growth trajectory of the region as a whole, as well as for individual countries within it, although an expanded focus on social assistance, regional development, and digital infrastructure is likely. We return to the impact of the global pandemic – and its opportunity to serve as a critical juncture – later in this chapter. Before that, we look at where exclusion is happening when it comes to innovation, and consider the challenges involved in achieving a more equitable spatial distribution of opportunity and benefits. In Box 4.1 Tanya Accone, Senior Adviser

Box 4.1 UPSHIFT: empowering a generation of change-makers

By Tanya Accone, UNICEF

From Indonesia to Vietnam, when young people have the space, time, and support, they turn to creative solutions to solve local challenges, most often tackling environmental and social problems in their communities.

UPSHIFT started in 2014 and focused on generating skills and jobs for young people facing high unemployment rates, especially those who were marginalized due to various intersectional factors such as disability, gender, ethnicity, economic marginalization, and their age. Seven years later, the UPSHIFT wave has lifted more than 1.3 million adolescents and young people across 35 countries – including Vietnam, Myanmar, and Indonesia – in which UNICEF has so far scaled the initiative.

In the program, young people have thought, done, failed, and tried again. Many have succeeded. In Vietnam, young people with disabilities have diagnosed and designed solutions for making their city more navigable, and put together services for employment preparation and job placement for fellow young people with disabilities. Others are experimenting with carbon-fighting algae to combat the carbon emissions from prevalent and polluting motorbikes, which are estimated to number 7.3 million in Ho Chi Minh City alone. These are ideas that have all made the journey from idea to reality, turning young people into social entrepreneurs who are changing the trajectory of their community one idea at a time.

The UPSHIFT approach is intentionally designed to tackle multiple aspects of what many young people experience as an entrenched and exclusionary innovation ecosystem. It makes use of the three elements of an inclusive innovation framework – the what, where, and how. UPSHIFT intentionally invests in and targets the participation of traditionally excluded and marginalized young people to acquire social innovation and entrepreneurship skills, to boost their confidence and competence to design solutions that solve social, economic, environmental, and climate-change-related vulnerabilities.

By seeking and incubating socially innovative ideas with adolescents and youth, young people act upon issues they care about and that have impact on their lives.

They are not alone. Each UPSHIFT program integrates itself into the local ecosystem. In Vietnam, this includes the relevant Ministries of Labour and Social Affairs (MOLISA) and Education (MOE), city governments such as the Ho Chi Minh City's Department of Science and Technology, national organizations like the Youth Union, key innovation ecosystem stakeholders such as the Saigon Innovation Hub,

and mentors and volunteers ranging from NGOs to private sector partners. Together with young people, it is this solidarity of stakeholders that
has realized the vision of integrating UPSHIFT as an extracurricular
activity in high schools and in the context of technical and vocational
education and training across the country including in the most remote
schools in the mountainous provinces of Dien Bien and Lao Cai, which
have a strong concentration of ethnic groups facing regular language
barriers to access quality educational content. The ambition in Vietnam
is to reach ten million adolescents and young people by 2026.

on Innovation at United Nations International Children's Emergency Fund
(UNICEF), shares the case of UPSHIFT, an initiative that is empowering
young entrepreneurs to tackle local challenges, across Southeast Asia.

Where is exclusion happening?

Inclusive innovation in a territorial sense points to measures to incentivize
the distribution of activities away from winning cities or clusters. The aim is
to buck the spatial determinism that comes with the emphasis on clusters as
centers of innovation, or as Marshallian districts. Yet this is at odds with contemporary patterns of innovation and the tendency it produces towards the
centralization of innovation activities. Florida and Hathaway (2018) analyzed
the vibrancy of the world's "startup cities." To do so, they examined more
than 100,000 venture deals across 300-plus global metro areas spanning 60
countries, from 2005 to 2017. On the basis of their findings, they assert that
we are seeing four transformations: (1) Great Expansion: a large increase in
the volume of venture deals and capital invested, (2) Globalization: growth
in startups and venture capital across the world, especially outside the USA,
(3) Urbanization: the concentration of startups and venture capital investment in large, globally connected cities, and (4) Winner-Take-All Pattern: with
the leading cities pulling away from the rest.

These transformations have created challenges as well as opportunities,
with many cities having become hotbeds of inequality and social challenges.
The "Winner-Take-All Pattern" is particularly worrying, as capital cities and
leading clusters of innovation become more detached from the region and
country in which they are based, leading to rising inequality. Regions that
are not already clusters of talent, finance capital, and operating according to
enabling social capital, struggle to join in innovation activities and so fall further behind high-performing regions.[32] As Guth asserts,

On the one hand innovation is necessary in order to enable regions to
economically catch up. On the other hand, innovations lead to further
redundancies and increasing disparities.[33]

Put another way, low-capacity regions would benefit from greater innovation activity in order to catch up, especially in terms of productive capacity, but that same application of innovation stands to cause short-term harm. There is a paradox to advances in regional innovation.[34] The advance of innovation – particularly automation or robotics – may cause job losses, which accentuate the socioeconomic challenges of the area. Innovation-induced redundancies can accentuate the issue in regions that already have high rates of unemployment and challenging social conditions. Thus, to "level up" abilities takes significant structural change, in terms of education provision, physical infrastructure, and more. In spatial terms, then, the losers of the innovation cycle are:

> regions which are unable to moderate the emergence of network or cluster structures – in short: regions where interactivity and inter-organizational learning does not take place.[35]

What's more, in order to effectively function as an innovation region, "a certain level of economic and social cohesion" is a "basic precondition."[36]

Exclusion related to spatial factors does not only take place in rural or remote areas, but can be observed in some urban settings as well. Focusing on precarious urban geographies as the location for analysis, Thieme conceives of a "hustle economy."[37] What Thieme means by hustle is that youth at the margins of the neoliberal economy in urban centers must hustle – engage in informal and precarious work – in order to get by. The hustle economy, in this way, places the urban setting as an arena for exclusion. Studies of inclusive innovation have reflected efforts to drive inclusion in innovation in urban, but socioeconomically disadvantaged, locations. Klingler-Vidra, for instance, found that French policies to increase participation in the production of innovation emphasize spatial criteria as a means of targeting citizens in low-income urban districts.[38] Socioeconomic disadvantage, then, can occur in both urban and rural settings, and so our study of inclusive innovation in geographic terms canvasses both arenas.

Exclusion happens within and between groups, as well as regions. As Westlund and Bolton explain, "by creating strong networks, actors/groups have shut others out from the resources and markets to which they have access."[39] The location of one's experience – whether in a home city or country, or across countries – has been found to act as an enabler and preclude in the context of innovation activities. Studies have found that scientific and technology-sector elite, especially coming from East and South Asia, have accumulated significant experience in the USA.[40] Klingler-Vidra et al. also find that transnational experience is prevalent amongst Vietnam's burgeoning set of high-performing tech founders.[41] They go on to explain that this stems from homophily and related effects, which mean that venture capitalists value Vietnamese returnees from the USA as they, themselves, are also either returnees or foreigners. This scholarship is valuable in the beginning to conceive of the ways in which social capital within systems can act in a negative way for particular groups, such as those who are unable to access transnational experience, particularly overseas education. The lack of this experience can act as a driver for underrepresentation in the context of innovation systems, including in high-technology entrepreneurship.

Migrant, refugee, and displaced communities are an interesting group to consider in the context of where innovation happens, and who is included or excluded from this process. Migration is typically regarded as a driver of innovation, through the transnational movement of knowledge, networks, and capital that it facilitates.[42] While transnational experience benefits highly-educated and experienced returnees and expats, migrants who have less social and finance capital struggle to realize the same benefits. Recognizing this, efforts to drive inclusion of migrant populations include the case of Learning Coin, which is an initiative started in 2020 to support marginalized children and youth with ethnic minority and stateless status. The initiative aims to provide a financial cash incentive, by turning reading into scholarships, so students remain in the education system and, at the same time, are able to help support their families. In this context, with over 670,000 children currently out of school in Thailand, obtaining an education is an opportunity-cost to families who are living at the margins. In response to this challenge, an organization designed and developed an inclusive program that is sensitive to such differences and contingencies. This does not express outbound innovation where the community members themselves directly craft their own solutions, yet they participate in a process that enables them to enhance their capability to improve their circumstances. The story of Learning Coin, in Box 4.2, offers an example of innovation aimed at including migrants.

Box 4.2 Learning Coin: scholarship, family, and becoming a "lifelong learner"

By Sowirin Chuanprapun, UNESCO

Several years ago, along the southern border of Thailand's Yala Province, 16-year-old Sofuwan had to drop out of school to urgently assist his parents. Sofuwan's father, a school janitor, was the pillar of financial support for the entire family. But back on the home front, Sofuwan's mother had recently lost her mobility due to a debilitating snake bite. From that moment onwards, Sofuwan's full-time assistance was needed if she was ever to recuperate properly.

Hence for over three years, Sofuwan would not be able to attend school like other children. Owing to the lack of good books at home and the long absence from his formal schooling, Sofuwan was finally not able to keep up with his reading skills. This led him to fear that he might never be able to realize his own purpose in life.

At the same time, and many miles north in Thailand's Mae Hong Son province, 17-year-old Jai Kham, a young Shan ethnic minority woman who had yet to obtain Thai citizenship, was also busy caring for family. With a passion for cooking, Jai Kham tried to earn regular income by selling Thai salad dishes and smoothies to the local community. To earn something extra, she worked as a waitress at a nearby restaurant every evening. Despite such a punishing workload, Jai Kham continued to possess a strong drive to study and, ultimately, to one day attend university.

Sofuwan and Jai Kham are among the over 670,000 children currently out of school in Thailand. Many of these children, like Sofuwan and Jai Kham, have to support their families in hard circumstances. For many of these young people, such conditions will all but certainly cost them their own schooling.

The "Learning Coin" project was conceived as an effort to help give young people like Sofuwan and Jai Kham the opportunity to earn income by turning reading into scholarships, so such students remain in the education system and, at the same time, are able to help support their families, all the while cultivating reading habits for lifelong learning.[43]

Since its inception in July 2020, the Learning Coin project has already supported 455 marginalized children and youth, many hailing from ethnic minority and stateless status. Learning Coin has helped them to read books from the content application "LearnBig" which is accessed on electronic tablets provided by the project. Students' daily reading efforts, including the number of reading hours spent, their reading consistency and answers submitted via the application, are all logged and analyzed with specific algorithms of the LearnBig system. These learning activities are calculated with a view towards producing monthly scholarships for their parents. Through their reading efforts, students can earn scholarships of up to 800–1,200 baht monthly (approximately US$26–40), which accounts for 10 percent of the average family income.

With the encouragement of his parents, Sofuwan has been able to further his study in a nonformal secondary education program at a community learning center in Bannang Sata. Since participating in the Learning Coin initiative, he has become one of the program's highest scholarship earners through his steady practice of reading. His mother has also played an important part in his progress, frequently inspiring him to read by helping to choose books from the LearnBig app.

"Reading helps me to become more knowledgeable," says Sofuwan, adding, "I was inspired [by Learning Coin] and wanted to continue to seek new knowledge." Sofuwan now reads almost every day after the morning Muslim prayer session. As he developed his Thai literacy skills, he also discovered a new passion for barista and latte art techniques through his learning journey.

While working multiple jobs, Jai Kham was enrolled in a nonformal secondary education program run by a district community learning center when she joined the Learning Coin program. The COVID-19 outbreak had cost her a great loss of income, and it has since forced the closure of her food stall for the foreseeable future.

"My dream is to own a restaurant," says Jai Kham. "I want to study culinary [arts] in order to do this business. I'm learning a lot from YouTube and also from on-the-job learning." Jai Kham has accumulated personal savings from reading books and is currently trying to open her shop again. The now 17-year-old woman continues to strive to overcome obstacles to running her own business and to follow her own dreams. No matter how hard she has had to work, however, she has remained committed to attending regular classes at the community learning center.

Through the 'Leaning Coin' program, teachers encourage youth to read books according to their current literacy levels. The program also awards students bonus points for measurable improvement each month, with an emphasis on acknowledging their individual learning achievements and reading efforts. Such measures contribute to supporting personalized approaches to learning and lending students further encouragement. So far, 15 learners with the highest scholarships have already spent between 21 and 95 hours monthly reading books on the platform.

Like any other technology-based project, the Learning Coin model has faced challenges in harnessing the use of technology among the most underprivileged target beneficiaries. Learning Coin has worked hard to develop both the system and the content that meets the needs of diverse users, as well as to design scholarship schemes and methods that continually motivate learning. A study by Chulalongkorn University (Bangkok) found that 45 percent of the children in the project have had to work various jobs to help their parents to earn the critically needed income. More than 88 percent of children lack the necessary tools for effective learning. Notably, nearly 35 percent of that number have no books in their homes other than textbooks. An effective reading scholarship approach demonstrates that the more frequently scholarships are made available, the more a child will be motivated to engage in constructive reading habits.

The success of the project would not have been possible without the dedication and attention of all participating teachers and volunteers, the student's own efforts and proper support provided by parents. "When I helped the children read, they made my day complete," says Duangrutai, a student volunteer from Chulalongkorn University. "I was very happy and wanted even more than ever to become a teacher."

Over the long term, UNESCO is seeking cooperation from other potential collaborators to bring blockchain technology to the project. This will enable the general public to get involved in cultivating marginalized children's reading habits and to support sustainable scholarship aid for such youth, including Jai Kham and Sofuwan themselves, who continue to strive to be educated for their immediate and long-term future.

Initiatives such as Learning Coin are making a difference, especially to those who participate directly. But there remains much to be done on the system level. This begs the question: if we know that innovation tends towards favoring in-groups and particular spatial clusters, why is it so difficult to create the conditions for a more equitable distribution of innovation's activities, and its benefits?

Where do policies strive for spatially inclusive innovation?

Innovation policies typically prioritize initiatives and programs designed to stimulate the development of high-growth potential sectors and regions, as well as investment in new or breakthrough technologies. It has traditionally been left to other areas of policy to deal with some of the negative externalities of economic growth, such as poverty, inequality, pollution, or the extraction and consumption of finite resources.

Local governments, close to local challenges in both urban and rural settings, have made advances in developing systems to drive inclusive innovation. The Seoul Innovation Park, for instance, is a physical space, opened in 2015 by the Seoul metropolitan government, that provides space for a variety of citizens and groups to think about social innovation in the same physical space. A "park for residents, a research center for innovators, and incubation space for young entrepreneurs," a "Youth Hub, Social Innovation Support Centre, Village Community Support Centre, and many other social innovation groups" are co-located there. Given the short time period since the innovation park was established (some of the buildings and projects were launched only in 2019), thus far, evidence of the benefits of co-location are anecdotal.[44] This is an emerging example of an increasing recognition of the role of local policy to "consider the social purpose of innovation, the distribution of its benefits and the roles (and power relationships) of those involved in innovation processes."[45] Yet even as place-based and "smart specialization" innovation strategies begin to proliferate,[46] there is no consensus about how best to support innovation that will lead to widely shared and sustainable development.

National governments have historically struggled to square the circle between high growth and distributed growth. A 2019 report for the World

Intellectual Property Organization observed that the countries with very successful national innovation strategies also tend to have a high degree of subnational concentration of innovation, wages, and incomes, and levels of interregional inequality that are higher than countries with less advanced NIS and policies. This is a striking finding, that,

> deliberate innovation or industrial policy frameworks have only rarely been able to both raise the national level of innovation and distribute it relatively evenly within the national territory.[47]

However, as noted in an overview of global startup cities, a failure to plan can also have unintended consequences. Speaking about the startup support ecosystem that has emerged in Nigeria, Adewale Yusuf, founder of technology media outlet Techpoint Africa, says, "Lagos happened not because it was intentionally planned. It happened out of necessity."[48]

Where planning does happen, it often draws heavily on models from innovation ecosystems that may not be locally relevant. As Breznitz argues in a study of how innovation happens in "real" places, the drive to recreate a Silicon Valley-styled model often leads policymakers to ignore constraints – and miss opportunities – to construct innovation ecosystems that are built on the talents, resources, and other advantages local areas have to offer.[49] This would allow areas to excel in the phase of the innovation process to which they are uniquely suited – from the early generation and design of new ideas, through the development, refinement, and production of products and services, and on to the usage, improvement, and scaling of these innovations. For Breznitz,

> the greatest opportunities for growth lie in communities' recognizing their own advantages, then fostering forms of specialized innovation that rely on those advantages.[50]

A 2021 study of the dynamics of entrepreneurial ecosystems concurs, noting that there is no one-size-fits-all approach to creating the perfect ecosystem, and that each place needs policies and an infrastructure tailored to its needs.[51] This kind of approach is starting to permeate mainstream innovation policy-making in Southeast Asia. An example of this is the aforementioned Inclusive Innovation Industrial Strategy being implemented by the government of the Philippines that aims, among other policy objectives, to create platforms that will support the emergence of local champions and leaders, and that will be "the medium in organizing, expanding, and mobilizing local communities of innovators and entrepreneurs."[52] For more on the role of policy, alongside multiple stakeholders, Rex Lor, at the UNDP Accelerator Lab for the Philippines, shares his insight into efforts to mainstream inclusive innovation in the country, as detailed in Box 4.3.

Box 4.3 Mainstreaming grassroots innovation in the Philippines

By Rex Lor, UNDP Philippines Accelerator Lab

The concept of grassroots innovation in the Philippines is not uncommon. Hacks, inventions, and innovations by ordinary citizens, especially the poor, are regularly featured both in mainstream and social media, often praising their ingenuity and resourcefulness. But despite the attention, strategic institutional support to these self-taught hackers and innovators is wanting. This is the context in which the partnership between the Department of Science & Technology Region XI (DOST XI) and the UNDP Philippines Accelerator Lab (UNDP ALabPH) is anchored: How might we identify and develop an ecosystem of support to enable regular citizens already innovating in their communities?

This aim saw the implementation of a partnership that launched more than eight solutions mapping "adventures" in the Davao Region (as of September 2021), training 200+ partners, and mapping 100+ grassroots innovations in both urban and rural communities. Together with DOST XI, the SalikLakbay Solutions Mapping Adventure, a localized version of the solutions mapping methodology of the global UNDP Accelerator Lab, has been successfully institutionalized within the GRIND program. Mappers, also called SalikLakbayers, search for user-led innovations that include tech hacks, sustainable livelihoods, indigenous technology and crafts, ethnobotanicals, heirloom recipes, nature-based solutions, and the like.

After more than a year of working with the DOST XI and grassroots innovators, several insights and lessons learned have been distilled from this collaborative undertaking:

1. The SalikLakbay Solutions Mapping activity builds on the theory that innovation is everywhere and people are inherently creative and innovative. For grassroots innovators, poverty is not a barrier but a motivation to better themselves, their family, and their community. DOST XI's experience in supporting grassroots innovators in rural areas saw that with the right mix of technical guidance, business coaching, and financial support, grassroots innovators can flourish and consequently boost the local economy. In Matanao, Davao del Sur, a Blaan tribal community reaps the benefits of a portable corn sheller, created by Demetrio Perez, a local farmer who loves to tinker and build agricultural machinery. His inspiration was borne out of the poverty he experienced in his community because people farm less crops as these are hard to manually process after harvest. His portable corn sheller provided a low-cost solution that allows his fellow farmers to process more corn and earn more from the

harvest. His innovative solutions drew the attention and support of the DOST XI where he was provided with technical support, training, and financing that allowed him to expand his business to cater more local farmers. (Watch: https://youtu.be/HI2sl-RRHVw)

2. Grassroots innovations from indigenous communities have a deep and special concern for the environment. Indigenous crafts, ethnobotanicals, and heirloom recipes mapped in the SalikLakbays with tribal communities emphasize the need for appreciation and protection of the environment. It is not just about taking what you need but more of a deep spiritual respect to the kinaiyahan (i.e. life in relation to the natural environment) – that by protecting the environment, the environment protects you and the community. Nanay Dalope of New Bataan, Davao de Oro, is the healer and weaver of the Mandaya tribe. The unique combination of medicinal plants and the raw materials they need for their weaves are all sourced from what local flora has to offer. As an elder, she recognizes the importance of protecting the environment as it is intrinsically linked to their culture and livelihood.

3. Grassroots innovators cannot exist in a silo and need the collective support of government, private sector, civil society, academia, and other sectors. If we are to level up grassroots innovations in the country from a mere curiosity to that of a legitimate pipeline of inventions and innovations that is worth investing in, there needs to be a framework and a structure to enable them.

In an uncertain time like the COVID-19 pandemic, grassroots innovators have been at the forefront of providing solutions in local Philippine communities. DOST XI acknowledges this in their report: "one the most effective ways to combat COVID-19 and the new normal is by promoting empowerment and building resilience among communities through the development and deployment of grassroots innovations." By broadening the scope and participation of innovation and making it more inclusive to all sectors (not just entrepreneurs and startups), we not only ensure more resilient communities but also empower the individuals that comprise these.

Where has COVID-19 acted as a critical juncture?

Crisis moments can generate innovative solutions. Such moments – when existing paradigms are questioned and there is new cognitive space for considering alternative approaches – are called "critical junctures." If we take COVID-19 as a critical juncture, the pandemic has the potential to diminish the power of clusters, particularly urban co-location. Less physical interaction since the onset of the pandemic potentially undermines the drivers of physical co-location that the Marshallian Trinity asserts. Teams can come together virtually, without being based in the same city or region, which could have a substantial impact on the accumulation of opportunity and economic gains in a geographic sense. In particular, strategies to further distribute innovation activities across rural regions – as in Vietnam's mountains and rural areas – could see more individuals and companies, particularly those participating in the knowledge economy, taking up residence.

COVID-19, though, also raised the value of a wide variety of urban-to-rural innovation paradigms. The story of ABC Bakery, whose founder acted fast to create a new product, pink bread, in order to offer a lifeline to farmers whose crops (beginning with dragon fruit) were going to waste. The story of the pink bakery movement is told by Berlin Tran, which is narrated in Box 4.4.

Box 4.4 ABC Bakery and the pink bakery movement

By Berlin Tran, Lecturer at the University of Economics Ho Chi Minh City

> I could clearly see the worry and sadness on their faces. It was desperation, like who could save us?

Kao Sieu Luc, a baker in Ho Chi Minh City, discovered that 300 containers of dragon fruit were stuck at the border with China, which was already closed due to the rising threat of the pandemic, in February 2020. Farmers had no choice but to discard their yield or sell at US$0.17 per kilo, a fifth the usual price.

Mr. Kao is a Vietnamese-Chinese baker who has worked and lived in Ho Chi Minh City for almost all of his life. The baker started his career in the 1970s as a rice and flour distributor, then in 1984 opened his own bakery, called Duc Phat, after his wife. Though not formally trained, Mr. Kao had a passion for baking and, especially through trial and error, taught himself a recipe repertoire of breads, cakes, and pastries from Europe and East Asia. In 2005, the bakery chain was renamed to ABC, after his three children, and started to export bread products to America, Europe, and Asia. Meanwhile, Mr. Kao was invited to the jury board of the Coupe du Monde de la Boulangerie, an international pastry competition, and became a member of the International Bakery Association. To the baker, however, commercial and professional success had never been his goal. Instead, he set himself a mission to develop Vietnamese baking by incorporating native ingredients and culinary expertise into international recipes (e.g. combining the French baguette with butterfly pea) and at the same time to bringing it to the world. Little did he know that the year 2020 would bring him another important mission.

On the 23rd of January 2020, Vietnam confirmed its first case of COVID-19, and although schools were shortly closed down, it was business as usual for all of the country's economic activity. It was also business as usual for Mr. Kao when, in February, he travelled to the Southwest to look for new ingredients and found that the situation for dragon fruit farmers was anything but usual. Witnessing firsthand the dire consequences of travel restrictions, he knew he had to do something to help. He felt the solution had to be more sustainable than simply buying a large amount of the fruit, despite its rock-bottom price at the time.

> I wondered how I could help. I could have bought two or three tonnes for my workers to enjoy, but at best that would have been a temporary fix. So, I was determined to find a solution for farmers.

Sustainability was his main concern because the baker himself used to farm in his youth. In our interview, Mr. Kao explained that he was aware of the "precarious nature" of farming, which was subjected to both "climate conditions and the market." Thus, the baker's sympathy with the "sweat and tears [that farmers] put in every yield" led him towards a social mission to save dragon fruit – and crucially, the livelihoods of the farmers.

Mr. Kao summoned an emergency meeting in the headquarters immediately following his trip. His proposed solution was that ABC Bakery would create new products which incorporated dragon fruit as a key ingredient, starting with the plain bread, and would then sell it at a low price to the public. This would enable the bakery chain to make and sell the bread in large quantities and therefore continuously procure dragon fruit on a substantial scale. Such a variety of bread had never been attempted before in Vietnam if not the world, at least on an industrial scale. Once work was delegated among the different departments of ABC, Mr. Kao and his R&D team got straight to developing the recipe for a dragon fruit bread. The recipe turned out to be not simple at all, partly because dragon fruit is high in water content and consequently prevents dough from rising. He and his team thus had to adjust the recipe repeatedly until the bread "passed [his] baking jury's taste." Finally, after three days of experimentation, the light-pink dragon fruit bread was ready for release.

We cared not for the promises of fame and fortune. The bread came from a sense of necessity and sharing, I should do it, we should do it. And helping farmers made us happy, so we carried on.

The pink bread was a success: 300 loaves were made as a pilot on the first day, and ABC Bakery advertised its new product on a banner in front of its stores, saying: "Save Vietnamese produce with ABC Bakery." All 300 were sold out, and the media – domestic and foreign – was quick to cover the pink banh mi (bread). The number of loaves rose to 3,000 after two days and then 40,000 after a week, but supply kept falling behind demand, with customers queuing for the pink break. At the same time, ABC's business clients, notably KFC, started to order products made with dragon fruit. This boosted the scale, as the amount of dragon fruit used by ABC Bakery rose from 200–300kg to 2.5 tonnes per day, and Mr. Kao was then procuring from whole villages. Nonetheless, the baker felt that his efforts alone "[were] not big enough in the big picture" and decided to share his recipe publicly so that

Anyone, any family could make the bread, small and large bakeries could make the bread. Many people could make it, the whole community actually, only then could we truly help farmers.

At the bottom of the recipe he even included his mobile number, so that anyone can call him if they struggled to replicate the recipe. This created a nationwide pink movement, where dragon fruit was bought by individuals and businesses to make not only bread and bread products, but also pho, noodles, rice paper, dumplings, and drinks. Two months after the first dragon fruit bread was sold, the price of dragon fruit recovered from US$0.17 to US$1.08 per kilo.

Mr. Kao did not stop at the dragon fruit bread during the pandemic. He also developed a special bread for frontline medical workers and any soldiers who operated quarantine facilities, who to him were "the most important people." The bread was made with whole grains and contained cheese, nuts, raisins, and honey, the amount and proportion of which was calculated by the baker in a way that "one or two slices would provide enough energy, protein, and other nutrients for medical workers [and quarantine soldiers] to keep going." All loaves made were donated to hospitals and quarantine facilities.

ABC Bakery's pink bread sparked a movement in favor of connecting urban consumers and rural farmers. It was not planned or centrally coordinated. Instead, an entrepreneur saw an opportunity to develop a new product as a means of being able to offer a domestic market to farmers in need, while purchasing supplies at a steep discount. It is an example of bridging the urban and rural, and operates at a logic different from the Marshallian Trinity. In the post-COVID-19 context, innovators and policymakers are asking what types of infrastructure could help facilitate this kind of innovation. Greater connectivity, in the form of internet access, is often raised as a means of providing a means for social networks to connect beyond their typical geographic patterns.

China is an interesting place to look for examples of how innovation in rural or remote areas can be stimulated, building on the rapid development of e-commerce platforms and the digital economy prompted by COVID-19. Since they were first established in 2009, China's "Taobao Villages" have benefited from the scale (and infrastructure) of national innovation production, by bringing rural villages into selling their goods (e.g. handicrafts) via Alibaba's e-commerce system. The corporate giant Alibaba, in collaboration with various levels of the Chinese government, has fueled the advance of Taobao Villages, which usher in the development of logistics infrastructure, digital literacy, and as a result, rural development.[53] A village is considered, by Alibaba, to be a Taobao Village when it constitutes "a cluster of rural electronic retailers where at least ten percent of village households engage in e-commerce and total annual e-commerce transaction volume in the village is at least ten million Chinese Yuan."[54] Alibaba, for its part, offers various online training programs to enable potential participants to sell via the platform.

Provincial governments enable online sales through investment in logistics infrastructure as well as skills upgrading, depending on the needs and resources of local producers. Wei et al. explain, for example, that "the Bureau of Transportation in Songyang County built an urban-rural logistics system with three large logistics companies to facilitate the rural e-commerce development in Xishan."[55] The Xishan model has been in decline, however, due to a lack of investment in innovation to upgrade production capacity. In other Taobao Villages, local governments have invested in capabilities development for the wooden toy industry, which have countered this challenge. For instance, the Qiaoyun local government "helped to build a Taobao industrial park in the village as an incubator and knowledge center."[56]

The potential for Taobao Villages, which foster "netrepreneurs," is enormous.[57] The model "can not only help rural areas develop distinctive industries, but also can promote employment opportunities in rural areas."[58] Following a similar logic, Pinduoduo launched in 2015 as a group-buying e-commerce platform. Pinduoduo is another interesting IT-enabled mechanism, as it enables consumers (largely based in lower-tier cities) to coordinate "team purchases" from smallholder farmers and handicraft producers in poverty-stricken villages in China. Similar to Taobao Villages, Pinduoduo collaborates with local governments and civil society in the communities where it operates. However, government relations have not all been positive; the Chinese government (more specifically, the State Administration for Market Regulation) has investigated Pinduoduo for its role in enabling the sales of imitation products and counterfeits.

We are only beginning to see the impacts of COVID-19 on innovation and development. Yet it offers an opportunity for all kinds of actors – from governments through to grassroots innovators – to think differently about the role of place, and to create new avenues for entrepreneurship and social innovation beyond the clusters and cities that have historically been dominant.

Who is involved in this approach, and how?

While efforts to distribute the spatial benefits of innovation are most often led by national governments as part of the implementation of industrial strategies, there are also key roles for other actors in the ecosystem to play in the "innovation everywhere" agenda, which we describe and illustrate through examples.

Academia can contribute to the development of innovative ideas and capabilities in rural or other disadvantaged areas through the application of subject matter expertise and the formation of local partnerships to drive innovation, or through direct provision of education and training. One example is the Medicinal Innovation for Red Dzao Ethnic Minority Community, developed by the Hanoi University of Pharmacy. The model involves the university helping the Red Dzao community to turn its traditional medicine into commercial products, working very closely together to put its interests and values at the center of the initiative. In doing so, Ngoc concludes that the university collaboration placed the community "into the whole value chain of herbal products," which "contributed to the benefit of very disadvantaged communities in mountainous areas."[59] Another example is the Pamulaan Center for Indigenous People's Education at the University of Southeastern Philippines, which was established in partnership with NGOs and state agencies in 2005 to provide education and training to indigenous young people, children, community leaders, and development workers. Included in the curriculum is a Bachelor of Science in Entrepreneurship.

Civil society may be involved in this approach by identifying challenges in rural or otherwise disadvantaged areas that require solving, and by supporting and connecting local innovators to financial or other kinds of assistance. For example, in 2010 the Hoi An's Women Union – with the support of the Global Environmental Facility (GEF) Small Grants Program and in partnership with the Vietnam Ministry of Natural Resources and Environment – piloted a program to collect, sort, and dispose of solid waste in Hoi An, a UNESCO World Heritage Site. Since then, the initiative has fostered both social and environmental innovation, bringing a group of previously excluded women from poor communities, and developing a model that has since been scaled to other regions in Vietnam.[60]

Funders and investors have a role to play in the more equitable distribution of innovation opportunities and capabilities by directing investments to areas and innovators that are not already well-served by the market. Recent years have seen a rise in impact investing, that is, investments that seek to achieve positive social and environmental impacts as well as financial returns. A 2018 report on the landscape of impact investing in Southeast Asia noted that these investors are often not physically located in the regions that they invest in, and further, that the concentration of ecosystem intermediaries in urban areas has limited the ability of social enterprises in rural areas to receive sufficient support.[61]

However, there are signs of change on this front. For instance, in 2018 the ASEAN Capital Markets Forum launched the ASEAN Social Bond Standards. Among other requirements, ASEAN Social Bond issuers must be based in the region, and proceeds must be directed to regional projects focused on basic infrastructure, essential services, affordable housing, job creation, food security, and socioeconomic development. As one example of this, Singapore-based company Impact Investment Exchange sold a US$8 million Women's Livelihood Bond in 2017 – the "first gender-related social bond listed on a stock exchange globally."[62] Proceeds have been channeled to microfinance initiatives in Cambodia and the Philippines, and social enterprises in Vietnam, to provide business funding to approximately 385,000 women.

Governments and international organizations have a central role to play in the coordination of efforts to spread innovation activities beyond urban areas or well-established innovation clusters. They often do so through direct funding or programs designed to create new industries or support for more traditional ones.[63] An example of this comes from Vietnam, and an S&T policy designed to broaden spatial participation in innovation called "development for developing rural areas, mountainous areas and ethnic minorities for the 2016–2020 period" (hereafter referred to as Rural Areas). In the Rural Areas program, the emphasis was on the transfer of technologies for agricultural contexts, such as crop growing, water treatment, and environmental protection. The program was the result of a collaboration across the Ministry of Science and Technology (MOST), the Ministry of Agriculture and Rural Development (MARD), the Vietnam Farmer's Union, and provincial organizations.[64] Ngoc observes that in the first six years of implementation, the Program transferred "856 technologies to rural, mountainous, and sea coastal areas, to backward and remote locations of ethnic minority communities."[65] In addition to this collaborative program, the MARD developed a website and information management system to gather and share information on crop maintenance with farmers.

Marta Pérez Cusó shares an overview of what UNESCAP Asia Pacific is doing to drive inclusive innovation across the Southeast Asian region. This is narrated in Box 4.5.

Grassroots innovators in remote, rural, or otherwise disadvantaged areas are central to the development of more inclusive forms of innovation that respond to, and are rooted in, the needs and experiences of different contexts. An example of this is the innovators supported by the Malaysian Foundation

---

Box 4.5 Promoting inclusive innovation at UNESCAP

By Marta Pérez Cusó, UNESCAP

The UN Economic and Social Commission for Asia and the Pacific (ESCAP) is supporting governments in the region to **formulate technology and innovation policies that support more inclusive outcomes**.

Since 2018, ESCAP has explored various means to promote more inclusive technology and innovation policies. This has involved promoting more inclusive policy design processes as well as encouraging more inclusive policies through specific inclusive objectives and through introducing an inclusive lens in policy design. ESCAP's work has involved:

- Introducing an inclusive lens in the formulation of national science, technology, and innovation policies in Cambodia and in Myanmar.
- Promoting inclusive business in ASEAN in collaboration with the inclusive Business Action Network.
- Supporting researchers to provide policy insight to governments on how to promote AI for social good through a partnership with Google and the Association of Asia-Pacific Rim Universities.
- Supporting policies that promote grassroots innovations, in collaboration with the Honey Bee Network and GIAN.
- Supporting the design of an inclusive national development strategy for "Mongolia in the Digital Age" in collaboration with the Pathways Commission.

In addition, UNESCAP has also promoted intergovernmental discussion on inclusive technology and innovation policies through a series of background notes, expert meetings, and official discussions. A key output of this work is the Frontiers of Inclusive Innovation report released in November 2021.[66]

---

for Innovation,[67] a grassroots innovation development agency that sits under the Ministry of Science, Technology and Innovation (MOSTI). The foundation runs a number of programs to scale and accelerate the development and diffusion of potential grassroots innovations in Malaysia, brokering collaborations with partners from government, industry, academia, and other civil society stakeholders. It focuses particularly on supporting innovative products developed by low-income groups.

Intermediary organizations such as accelerators or incubators have a major role to play in supporting the development of innovation capabilities in peripheral areas. They are embedded within local innovation ecosystems and, as such, have a much deeper understanding of the needs and potential of those they support than central government policymakers. They can provide more tailored support, and can also be a conduit to aggregate and communicate the needs of local innovators to those with the power to make policy or investment decisions. For example, Support Her Enterprise (SHE)[68] is a Cambodian social enterprise that delivers gender-focused business incubator and accelerator programs for micro-small enterprises. It works in partnership with NGOs, local and international organizations, businesses, and governments with the aim of building an effective enterprise support ecosystem for women in Cambodia.

Large firms in Southeast Asia, given their influence and capacity, have the potential to foster and promote inclusive innovation across regions. By knowing what to prioritize, they can make participation in the production of innovation more inclusive by employing staff across regions and demographics. They can also orient towards a more spatial understanding of consumers, across a wider range of geographies, particularly underserved consumers. As an illustration of the potential of big firms to contribute, in 2020, Viettel – the largest telecommunications service provider in Vietnam – presented 178 remote healthcare consultation centers, worth VND 19 billion, to the Ministry of Health, in the hope of improving healthcare for both troops and people across the country.[69] The goal of these remote consultation centers is to provide health counseling, timely diagnosis and treatment, and quality medical services for all people regardless of where they live. Moreover, doctors at the district level can receive regular and ad hoc expertise from doctors at other hospitals by utilizing information technology platforms. The aim is to help increase the efficiency of disease prevention and control, reduce overcrowding at city- and province-level hospitals, and raise the quality of medical examination and treatment for people.

Startups and SMEs play a role in this approach to inclusive innovation by being rooted in. or by developing, solutions for regions and communities that are otherwise not well served by innovation. As Quaggiotto asserts, for a long time the development sector has been dominated by international financial institutions, development organizations, and large global NGOs.[70] However, the relevance and dominance of these institutions has in recent years been challenged by a host of startups, social enterprises, and informal self-organized collectives that are adept at uncovering locally relevant solutions.

A good example of this is Local Alike, a social enterprise that has grown across Thailand and focuses on responsible, community-based tourism with a unique benefit distribution and cross-sector collaboration model. It has partnerships with over 50 companies and focuses its efforts on providing locals with employment opportunities across 46 Thai provinces. It does this by providing unforgettable experiences to tourists interested in supporting local communities through community-based tourism. Local Alike's CEO, Somsak Boonkam, believes that tourism activities can be said to be sustainable only if they *enhance* local businesses and jobs, not if they *replace* them.

Somsak organizes training to ensure local tour guides are self-sufficient and are computer literate entrepreneurs. Some of the skills acquired include determining local carrying capacity, transforming local stories into meaningful and competitive tour packages, resource-finding and management, using online tools for sales and marketing, and identifying issues of concern to change and then marketize. In recognition of its innovative approach, in 2016, the Thai government proposed policy support for community-based tourism and awarded Local Alike with the responsibility of creating a model that can be applied to sustainable tourism business enterprises.

Strengths and shortcomings

An "everywhere" approach to innovation that is grounded in spreading innovative opportunities, capabilities, and benefits to remote or otherwise disadvantaged areas offers, in principle, a systematic means of creating regional development and greater shared prosperity. The degree to which these benefits are realized will likely depend on the form they take in practice. If the new industries and sectors promoted through "Innovation everywhere" type initiatives create a significant number of new, good-quality jobs, and if there are strong linkages between them and other parts of local economies (e.g. if they are based on the processing of local resources), there is reason to believe that they may offer significantly shared benefits in traditionally neglected regions.

However, if the promoted industries are highly capital intensive, creating few jobs, and if they lack any significant meaningful connections to other parts of the local economy, it is unlikely that their benefits will be shared widely beyond a narrow elite of politicians, researchers, and business owners. If the new industry in question is heavily polluting to the local environment, this may also undermine its potential benefits for the population. How inclusive this approach to innovation really is, then, will depend much on the types of industry and products which receive attention and support, which in turn draws attention to 'how' innovation is pursued in an inclusive manner and the extent to which it engages with appropriate technologies.

Notes

1 Francis Mark A. Quimba, Jose Ramon G. Albert, and Gilberto M. Llanto, "Innovation activity of firms in the Philippines." Discussion Papers DP 2017-44, *Philippine Institute for Development Studies.* December 2017.
2 Raj Chetty, Nathaniel Hendren, Patrick Kline, Emmanuel Saez, and Nicholas Turner, "Is the United States still a land of opportunity? Recent trends in intergenerational mobility." *American Economic Review* 104, no. 5 (2014): 141–147.
3 Alex Bell, Raj Chetty, Xavier Jaravel, Neviana Petkova, and John Van Reenen, "Who becomes an inventor in America? The importance of exposure to innovation." *NBER Working Papers 24062*, National Bureau of Economic Research.

4 Alfred Marshall, *Principles of Economics* (London and New York: Macmillan, 1890).

5 Fiorenza Belussi and Katia Caldari, "At the origin of the industrial district: Alfred Marshall and the Cambridge School." *Cambridge Journal of Economics* 33, no. 2 (2009): 335–355.

6 Gilles Duranton and William R. Kerr, "The logic of agglomeration." *NBER Working Paper Series,* No. 21452, NBER: Cambridge, MA. August 2015.

7 Michael E. Porter, "Clusters and the new economics of competition." *Harvard Business Review* November–December (1998): 78.

8 Bruce Katz and Julie Wagner, "The rise of innovation districts: a new geography of innovation in America." *Brookings Institute*, May 2014.

9 See Yigitcanlar et al. (2020) for a more detailed review of classifications and characteristics of innovation districts. Tan Yigitcanlar, Rosemary Adu-McVie, and Isil Erol, "How can contemporary innovation districts be classified? A systematic review of the literature." *Land Use Policy* 95 (C).

10 Jerome S. Engel, Jasmina Berbegal-Mirabent, and Josef M. Pique, "The renaissance of the city as a cluster of innovation." *Cogent Business & Management* 5, no. 1 (2018): 2.

11 Jerome S. Engel, "What are clusters of innovation, how do they operate and why are they important?" in *Global Clusters of Innovation: Entrepreneurial Engines of Economic Growth around the World,* Jerome S. Engel (ed) (Cheltenham: Edward Elgar, 2014).

12 Eric Weiner, *Geography of Genius: A Search for the World's Most Creative Places from Ancient Athens to Silicon Valley* (New York: Simon & Schuster, 2016).

13 Weiner, *Geography of Genius,* 324.

14 Bengt-Åke Lundvall, *National Systems of Innovation: Toward a Theory of Innovation and Interactive Learning* (London: Pinter, 1992); Richard R. Nelson, *National Systems of Innovation: A Comparative Analysis* (New York: Oxford University Press, 1993).

15 Stephen B. Adams, "From orchards to chips: Silicon Valley's evolving entrepreneurial ecosystem." *Entrepreneurship & Regional Development* 33, no. 1–2 (2021): 15–35.

16 Bing Xu, Haijing Yu, and Lili Li, "The impact of entrepreneurship on regional economic growth: a perspective of spatial heterogeneity." *Entrepreneurship & Regional Development* 33, no. 3–4 (2021): 309–331.

17 Engel, Berbegal-Mirabent, and Pique, "The renaissance of the city as a cluster of innovation," 2.

18 Jane Marceau, "Introduction: innovation in the city and innovative cities." *Innovation: Management, Policy & Practice* 10 (2008): 138.

19 OECD, *Innovation in Southeast Asia.* OECD Reviews of Innovation Policy (OECD Publishing, Paris, 2013). https://doi.org/10.1787/9789264128712-en.

20 Ridhma Dhar, *Innovation in South and South East Asia.* Clarivate Derwent. 2020. https://img06.en25.com/Web/ClarivateAnalytics/%7Bd46a600a-335e-4a96-b87b-149413edc15a%7D_DW554309991_Innovation_in_South___South_East_Asia.pdf.

21 Richard Florida, "Does urbanization drive Southeast Asia's development?" *Bloomberg.* January 18, 2017. https://www.bloomberg.com/news/articles/2017-01-18/how-urbanization-is-driving-southeast-asia-s-economies.

22 McKinsey and Company, *Smart Cities in Southeast Asia.* Discussion Paper. July 2018.   https://www.mckinsey.com/~/media/mckinsey/business%20functions/ope rations/our%20insights/smart%20cities%20in%20southeast%20asia/mgi-smart-cities-in-southeast-asia.pdf.

23 McKinsey and Company, *Smart Cities in Southeast Asia,* 3.

24 OECD, *Southeast Asia Going Digital: Connecting SMEs* (OECD, Paris, 2019). www.oecd.org/going-digital/southeast-asia-connecting-SMEs.pdf.

25 Cornell University, INSEAD, and WIPO, *The Global Innovation Index 2020: Who Will Finance Innovation?* (Ithaca, Fontainebleau, and Geneva, 2020).

26 Masahito Ambashi, "Innovation policy in/for ASEAN" in *The ASEAN Economic Community Into 2025 and Beyond,* Rebecca Sta. Maria, Shujiro Urata, and Ponciano S. Intal, Jr. (eds) (ASEAN@50, Vol. 5. Economic Research Institute for ASEA and East Asia, 2017), 213–232. www.eria.org/ASEAN_50_Vol_5_ Complete_Book.pdf.

27 Dhar, *Innovation in South and South East Asia.*

28 CIEM, British Council, United Nations Economic and Social Commission for Asia and the Pacific, and Social Enterprise UK, *Social Enterprise in Vietnam.* Hanoi. March 2019.

29 Randy Spence, "Research councils and support organizations in Southeast Asia: institutions, issues and collaboration." *International Development Research Center.* November 2008, p. 7.

30 Ca Tran Ngoc, "Universities and inclusive innovation for development: concepts and practices in Vietnam" in *Universities, Inclusive Development and Social Innovation,* Claes Brundenius, Bo Göransson, and Jose Manoel Carvalho de Mello (eds) (Cham: Springer, 2016), 258.

31 Ateneo School of Government, "Universities and councils network on innovations for inclusive development in Southeast Asia (UNIID-SEA): project brief." https:// ateneo.edu/sites/default/files/Project%20Brief%20-%20UNIID-SEA.pdf.

32 Phllip Cooke, "Regional innovation, entrepreneurship and talent systems." *International Journal of Entrepreneurship and Innovation Management* 7, no. 2/3/4/ 5 (2007): 117–139.

33 Michael Guth, "Innovation, social inclusion and coherent regional develop-ment: a new diamond for a socially inclusive innovation policy in regions." *European Planning Studies* 13, no. 2 (2005): 334.

34 Christine Oughton, Mikel Landabaso, and Kevin Morgan, "The regional innov-ation paradox: innovation policy and industrial policy." *The Journal of Technology Transfer* 27, no. 1 (2002): 97–110.

35 Guth, "Innovation, social inclusion and coherent regional development," 336.

36 Guth, "Innovation, social inclusion and coherent regional development," 338.

37 Tatiana Adeline Thieme, "The hustle economy: informality, uncertainty and the geographies of getting by." *Progress in Human Geography* 42, no. 4 (2017): 529–548.

38 Klingler-Vidra, *Global Review of Diversity and Inclusion in Business Innovation.*

39 Westlund and Bolton, "Local social capital and entrepreneurship," 81.

40 Bat Batjargal, "Internet entrepreneurship: social capital, human capital, and per-formance of internet ventures in China." *Research Policy* 36 (2007): 605–618; Martin Kenney, Dan Breznitz, and Michael Murphree, "Coming back home after the sun rises: returnee entrepreneurs and growth of high-tech industries." *Research Policy* 42, no. 2 (2013): 391–407; John Gibson and David McKenzie, "Scientific

mobility and knowledge networks in high emigration countries: evidence from the Pacific." *Research Policy* 43 (2014): 1486–1495.

41 Klingler-Vidra, Tran, and Chalmers, "Transnational experience and high-performing entrepreneurs in emerging economies."

42 Anna D'Ambrosio, Sandro Montresor, Mario Davide Parrilli, and Francesco Quatraro, "Migration, communities on the move and international innovation networks: an empirical analysis of Spanish regions." *Regional Studies* 53, no. 1 (2019): 6–16; Annakatrin Niebuhr, "Migration and innovation: does cultural diversity matter for regional R&D activity?" *Papers in Regional Science* 89, no. 3 (2010): 563–585.

43 Funded by the Equitable Education Fund Thailand, UNESCO Bangkok has been implementing the Learning Coin initiative together with the Thai Ministry of Education; 79 teachers at 53 Thai public schools and community learning centers; 273 student volunteers of Chulalongkorn University's Faculty of Education; the Mercy Centre; the Foundation for the Better Life of Children; and True Corporation. UNESCO Bangkok is committed to developing the program further in order for this low-investment, inclusive educational innovation model to continue to have impact.

44 UNDP Vietnam, *Inclusive Innovation Policy for the Next Development Stage,* 23.

45 Stanley, Glennie, and Gabriel, "How inclusive is innovation policy?" 8.

46 For more, see Ugo Fratesi, Carlo Gianelle, and Fabrizio Guzzo, *Assessing Smart Specialization: Policy Implementation Measures* (Luxembourg: Publications Office of the European Union, 2021).

47 Riccardo Crescenzi, Simona Iammarino, Carolin Ioramashvili, Andrés Rodríguez-Pose, and Michael Storper, *The Geography of Innovation: Local Hotspots and Global Innovation Networks.* (Word Intellectual Property Organization. Economic Research Working Paper No. 57, November 2019), 13.

48 Rest of World, "Beyond Silicon Valley." July 16, 2021. https://restofworld.org/2021/beyond-silicon-valley/.

49 Dan Breznitz, *Innovation in Real Places: Strategies for Prosperity in an Unforgiving World* (Oxford: Oxford University Press, 2021).

50 Breznitz, *Innovation in Real Places,* 5.

51 David Audretsch, Colin Mason, Morgan P. Miles, and Allan O'Connor, "Time and the dynamics of entrepreneurial ecosystems." *Entrepreneurship & Regional Development* 33, no. 1–2 (2021): 1–14.

52 Department of Trade and Industry, "Inclusive Filipinnovation and Entrepreneurship Roadmap." *Government of Philippines* (2019). http://innovate.dti.gov.ph/resources/i3s-strategy/inclusive-filipinnovation-and-entrepreneurship-roadmap/.

53 Anthony H.F. Li, "E-commerce and Taobao villages. A promise for China's rural development." *China Perspectives* 3, no. 1 (2017): 57–62.

54 Felix Ter Chian Tan, Shan Ling Pan, and Lili Cui, "IT-enabled social innovation in China's Taobao villages: the role of netrepreneurs." *Paper presented at the Thirty Seventh International Conference on Information Systems, Dublin.* December 11–14, 2016, p. 2.

55 Yehua Dennis Wei, Juan Lin, and Ling Zhang, "E-commerce, Taobao villages and regional development in China." *Geographical Review* 110, no. 3 (2020): 395.

56 Wei, Lin, and Zhang, "E-commerce, Taobao villages and regional development in China," 396.

57 For more on netrepreneurs see Joseph Lowery, Johnny Jackson, and Marcia Layton Turner, *Netrepreneur: The Dimensions of Transferring Your Business Model to the Internet* (Que Corp., 1998).
58 Lifang Peng, Jen-Her Wu, Yi-Cheng Chen, and Chun Cheng, "The performance and value creation of e-commerce ecosystems in rural China: a perspective of systems theory." *PACIS* (2019), 2.
59 Ngoc, "Universities and inclusive innovation for development," 275.
60 Vishal Gulati, "How waste management is helping Vietnamese women earn a living." *Earth Journalism Network*. July 5, 2018. https://earthjournalism.net/stor ies/how-waste-management-is-helping-vietnamese-women-earn-a-living.
61 Global Impact Investing Network and Intellecap, *The Landscape for Impact Investing in Southeast Asia*. August 2, 2018. https://thegiin.org/research/publicat ion/landscape-southeast-asia.
62 Yohei Kitano, "Social impact investing looks set to rise in ASEAN." *Nomura*. December 2020. www.nomuraconnects.com/focused-thinking-posts/social-impact-investing-looks-set-to-rise-in-asean/.
63 For the history of the role of the state in boosting venture capital markets, in order to finance innovation, in East Asia, see Robyn Klingler-Vidra, *The Venture Capital State: The Silicon Valley Model in East Asia* (Ithaca, NY: Cornell University Press, 2018).
64 MOST. *Report on Program for Science and Technology Development for Rural and Mountainous Areas* (Hanoi: MOST, 2012); NISTPASS, *Toward an Evolving Innovation System in Agriculture. Case of Three Products: Vegetable/Fruits, Tea, and Shrimp in Vietnam* (Hanoi: Science and Technics, 2011).
65 Ca Tran Ngoc, "Universities and inclusive innovation for development: concepts and practices in Vietnam," 264.
66 To access the UNESCAP *Frontiers of Inclusive Innovation* report. www.unescap. org/kp/2021/frontiers-inclusive-innovation-formulating-technology-and-innovation-policies-leave-no-one.
67 Details on the Malaysian Innovation Foundation can be found here: www.yim. my/ms/.
68 More information about SHE is available here: www.sheinvestments.com/.
69 Minh Thi, "Viettel trao tặng 178 trung tâm hội chẩn từ xa cho Bộ Y tế." *The Socialist Republic of Vietnam Online Newspaper of the Government*, September 24, 2020. http://baochinhphu.vn/Doanh-nghiep/Viettel-trao-tang-178-trung-tam-hoi-chan-tu-xa-cho-Bo-Y-te/408497.vgp
70 Giulio Quaggiotto, "Profiling the international development mutants." *Nesta*. May 17, 2017. www.nesta.org.uk/blog/profiling-the-international-development-mutants/.
71 Authors' reproduction of Ambashi, 2017. Note the * next to Myanmar, reflecting political developments in 2021.

5   The future of inclusive innovation

This chapter connects the vibrant cases of inclusive innovation in practice – as covered in Chapters 2 through 4 – with state-of-the-art literature on inclusive innovation in Southeast Asia and beyond. It details the concept and maps out the various ways in which inclusive innovation has manifested in policy and community-driven forms, responding back to the practices discussed in the three preceding chapters.

As we have argued and illustrated throughout the book, inclusive innovation involves a wide range of technologies (from social innovation through to low-tech to ICT), constitutes new forms of innovation by multiple stakeholders, and involves problem-owners as problem-solvers in addressing environmental and social challenges. Our conceptualization of inclusive innovation according to "how," "what," and "where" aims to capture this range of efforts.

In this chapter, we also examine the future of inclusive innovation, particularly in Southeast Asia. We strive to unpack the gaps and solidify the working understanding of the concept of inclusive innovation as it is evolving. Based upon this, we also offer a view for the way ahead, in the post-pandemic recovery and under the heading of "building back better," as in the UN's 2020 *Human Development Report.*[1] We close with a call to action for building the bridge between policy, practice, and theory.

Revisiting the concept of inclusive innovation

The myriad promises, and understandings, of inclusive innovation have led to the development of numerous approaches that consider the environmental and social purposes of innovation, the distribution of its benefits, and the roles and power relationships of those involved. In this brief section, we distil three themes that animate the proliferation of inclusive innovation, and the understanding of inclusive innovation, as articulated in the scholarship:

DOI: 10.4324/9781003125877-5

Table 5.1 Inclusion in terms of the production and consumption of innovation

	Production: *inclusion in innovation process*	Consumption: *use of innovation to aid social inclusion*
Aim	To increase the inclusion of underrepresented groups as producers of innovation activities.	To encourage the consumption of innovations in order to ameliorate social challenges faced by particular groups.
Target criteria	Ascriptive groups / demographics, disadvantaged socioeconomic regions / spatial determinants, traditional industries.	Disabled people, base-of-the-pyramid, traditional industry, rural populations.
Examples	Enable Code.	DMap, Liter of Light.

Source: Adaption based upon authors' review of extant literature.[2]

1. Production versus consumption orientation

As mentioned briefly earlier, an oft-cited conceptualization of inclusive innovation posits a dichotomy such that inclusion can either be about "producers" or "consumers" of innovation.[3]

Producer-oriented strategies aim to activate more segments of society as creators of innovation. This fits well with our notion of the inclusive innovation problem-owners also being the problem-solvers. Consumption-focused initiatives, comparatively, focus on encouraging the development of technologies, business practices, or services in order to solve social challenges for particular demographic groups, such as applying innovation to agriculture in order to improve crop production and benefit farmers. This can also emphasize innovation for a wider set of challenges and contexts, especially by those experiencing it. We depict the consumer-producer binary in Table 5.1, in terms of the aims, target criteria, and examples.

Vulcan Augmetics, as noted previously, offers an example of an inclusive innovation that is oriented towards an underserved consumer group (amputees in Vietnam) *and* aims to improve the job prospects of its users. The Ho Chi Minh City-based startup makes prosthetics using 3D printing technology to make affordable, modular prosthetics in, and for, the Vietnamese market.[4] Founded by Rafael Masters and Akshay Sharma, Vulcan offers specialist prosthetic models for improving the range of employment opportunities for amputees. The prosthetics are affordable and modular for particular tasks, such as being able to work as a waiter. The challenge they solve is that prosthetics are often one-size-fits-all models that allow very little customization and often come at a high cost.

2. Criteria according to demographic, spatial, and industrial characteristics

Inclusive innovation typologies have also distilled efforts according to who, how and where they are being targeted;[5] in this book, we advanced an

Table 5.2 OECD (2017) inclusive innovation framework

	Demographic	*Industrial*	*Spatial*
Target beneficiaries	Ascriptive traits, such as age, disability, ethnicity, gender, race, and sexuality.	Industry or sector.	Region or territory.
Rationale	Marginalization, underrepresentation, or exclusion in innovation activities based upon demographic characteristics.	Productivity gap across industries or sectors due to relative engagement or use of technological applications.	Geographic unevenness in the production and consumption of innovation activities, particularly across urban/rural dichotomies.

Source: Authors' understanding.[6]

approach that also analyzes the "what" dimension, particularly the development and use of technological innovation for social and environmental good.

Typologies such as those advanced by Planes-Satorra and Paunov in their OECD report on inclusive innovation policies are primarily interested in the who, or the destination, rather than the how or the what.[7] Demographically-motivated efforts point to ascriptive groups, meaning those disadvantaged according to factors assigned by birth, not achievement, such as gender, age, and minority or ethnic status.[8] Spatial efforts aim to diminish the gap between urban/rural, wealthy/poor, and core/periphery. The third domain is that of promoting innovation in traditional industry, which strives to infuse technological innovations or socially innovative approaches into firms' production processes. The OECD's 2017 framework, by Planes-Satorra and Paunov, distils inclusive innovation efforts into these three arenas: demographic/social, industrial/sectoral, and spatial/geographic, as illustrated in Table 5.2.

3. Distinct – rather than joined-up or intersectional – efforts across governments

Within the government, inclusive innovation policies have been initiated by numerous ministries, sometimes without coordination across government agencies, and not in cooperation with private sector, local communities and civil society groups. Ministries of Social Affairs and Education, for instance, act by way of active labor market policies, skills training, benefits transfer, and redistribution more broadly.[9] Ministries of Science and Technology, without linking with the Social Affairs initiatives, strive to craft "distribution-sensitive innovation policy," in which R&D budgets are more dispersed, in demographic and spatial terms, across society. The net result is that governments have an opportunity to better leverage their myriad policies to promote more inclusive innovation across society.[11]

Helping to operationalize the study of inclusive innovation, especially from a policy perspective, the 2018 Nesta framework contends that innovation policies may be inclusive if they are concerned with the direction, participation, and/or governance of innovation. Table 5.3 distills the description, core questions, and indicators that comprise the framework.

The indicators specified in the Nesta framework help to operationalize one's assessment of the extent to which an initiative – especially a policy – is inclusive. The EY STEM app, which gamifies STEM education in order to boost young women's engagement and skills, offers a good example of sparking interest and ability at a crucial age. Rohan Malik, who helped lead the EY STEM app's rollout in India, shares his story here, which is provided in Box 5.1.

Table 5.3 Nesta (2018) inclusive innovation policy framework

	Description	Core questions	Indicators
1. Direction	Ways in which distributive implications are considered.	Do the overall aims involve more than economic growth? Whose needs are being met?	1.1 Objectives are not exclusively related to economic growth, but take account of a wider range of socially desirable outcomes, such as sustainability, equality, health, and well-being. 1.2 Support for innovation addressing "societal" challenges and needs. 1.3 Support for innovation addressing the particular needs of excluded groups.
2. Participation	How inclusion is operationalized and for whom.	Who participates in innovation?	2.1 Measures to increase the participation of underrepresented and excluded social groups in innovation and innovative sectors of the economy. 2.2 Measures to increase the participation of disadvantaged or lagging regions or districts. 2.3 Measures to promote innovation in low-productivity or low-innovation sectors. 2.4 Measures to involve civil society and social economy organizations in innovation.

Table 5.3 Cont.

	Description	Core questions	Indicators
3. Governance	Process for involving wider society in governance.	Who sets priorities, and how are the outcomes of innovation managed?	3.1 Measures to broaden participation in innovation priority-setting. 3.2 Measures to broaden participation in the regulation of innovation. 3.3 Measures to mitigate the risks of innovation. 3.4 Measures to promote fair distribution of the benefits of innovation.

Source: Authors' understanding of the Nesta (2018) framework.[10]

The Nesta framework begins with the direction, which speaks to the ways, and extent, to which distributive implications are considered. The directional considerations are followed by participation, which speaks to the operationalization of this, in terms of who, specifically benefits. To apply this aspect of the framework, one may consider the precise criteria specified by the service or policy. If the aim is socioeconomically disadvantaged areas, how is that defined? In terms of income level, or in terms of a specific district, city, or region? Finally, the questions about governance then come back to the ways in which the initiative involves wider society in the management of the efforts. This includes agenda-setting, measurement, and distilling lessons learned.

Our framework, as advanced in this book, builds on these debates and concepts, by conceiving of inclusive innovation approaches in the following ways:

1. **How: innovation by and for the problem-owners** is a mix of top-down and bottom-up activities seeking to improve the quality of life and work for those in the most disadvantaged and marginalized communities (i.e. supporting the development of contextually-relevant innovations that address some of the root causes of poverty and inequality); problem-owners are also, often, the problem-solvers.
2. **What: innovation for environmental and social good** is mostly bottom-up, yet inclusive of larger-scale initiatives seeking to develop technological solutions to environmental and societal challenges (i.e. directing innovation towards achieving inclusive outcomes).
3. **Where: innovation everywhere** is mostly top-down government initiatives seeking to ensure that high-value, innovative activities are regionally distributed (i.e. encouraging the participation of more people, places, and sectors in the innovative economy).

The three approaches – in terms of these key questions – are the "how" (process and people-centered innovation), "what" (specifically, technology), and the "where" (geographic distribution).

Through our how, what, and where approach, we contend that the future of inclusive innovation needs to place (1) people *and* planet at the center of the objectives, (2) go beyond information technology, and the ideal of Silicon Valley, in conceiving of technological innovation, and (3) enable problem-owners to include themselves in innovation as problem-solvers, rather than having to wait for this opportunity to be offered to them by others. We began with the "who," in establishing who is included and who owns the problem. The consideration of who, which takes stock of the interdependent relationship between humanity, nature, and the environment, features across the framework and the various chapters. We then put the "how" before the medium, or the "what" of technological innovation. We underscore the argument that the social aims of inclusive innovation, including in its BoP roots, must evolve to take intersectionality with the environment into account. This is owing to the urgency of the climate crisis and acknowledgment that those who are most economically vulnerable are also those most at risk to the perils of climate change.

A key similarity between these three expressions of inclusive innovation is their focus on creating value and opportunities with, and for, those who face structural disadvantages in becoming either consumers or producers of innovation. This applies to places, people, and sectors of the economy who are often neglected in discussions of "frontier technologies" or the Fourth Industrial Revolution (IR4.0).

These types of outcomes are not always prioritized by mainstream innovation policies, which are often more focused on reinforcing existing national strengths and centers of excellence, rather than democratizing access to the power, knowledge, and tools needed to innovate. There is inspiration to be taken here for innovation policymakers everywhere, placing the aims of local context and the environment, as in Schumacher, on par with the growth-centric aims of Schumpeter.

Box 5.1 EY STEM app: an innovator's learning journey

By Rohan Malik, EY STEM app, Ernst and Young

For nearly two years after graduating from university in London, I felt like I had the best job in the world. Working as a Strategy Consultant at Ernst & Young's growing Education practice meant I had the opportunity to solve important challenges in education for the central government, state governments, the UN, think tanks, and foundations. I could, for a certain amount of time, help solve a problem alongside people. Over time though, the glamour of the names started to fade, and it began to be the problems I was helping clients solve that stuck with me. Some of them were problems I knew and cared deeply about before the first meeting – technology for social good, equity in education, and upskilling teachers. Others, I didn't know the extent of – teacher micro-innovations in classrooms with scarce resources, the power of technical education for a young population, and issues with how data was collected. But there was one cause that was overlooked, pressing, and had many nuances within it – the gender gap in technology.

After working as a client-facing consultant on a growth path that would have led to promotions, raises, and eventually an MBA, I took the decision to possibly give all that up and align myself full-time to EY's Women in Technology movement. For the first time, my purpose felt a lot greater than just working to solve a problem alongside a client for a finite period. This felt larger than a project; it was a "movement." From very structured teams where each member was an important "resource" whose time was billed by the hour, I was working with an incredible team of men and women all over the world working towards one common societal goal. Suddenly, the value of my time was not determined by my expertise in a certain area, but the impact of my ideas. Upon reflection, the entire team involved in the innovation felt a shift once they had this realization.

One of the pillars of the global Women in Technology movement, sponsored by the Chairman and leadership at EY, was the Educate pillar. This aimed to tackle the gender gap in technology at the stage when biases begin to dissuade girls from careers in STEM – biases, misconceptions, a lack of awareness or incentives to step out of their curricular comfort zones and explore applied content from leading thinkers. With this, I was fortunate enough to help design, build, pilot, and now scale EY STEM app.

EY STEM app (formerly EY STEM Tribe) is an innovative, gamified, and free platform for girls aged 13–18 that aims to identify, inspire, and empower the next generation. We built the platform with Tribal Planet, a Silicon Valley–based technology company driven by social good. To spark engagement, cross collaboration and to scale globally, the program created an ecosystem of governments, content providers, schools, nonprofits, corporations, teachers, and caregivers to create an environment of support for girls. The app itself incentivizes a learning model that has over 17 content channels and 450+ activities that are divided into channels such as Exploring Technology, Mysteries of Science, Designing our World, Natural World, Jobs of the Future, Getting Creative, Understanding Myself, and Helping the World. All the content is agnostic to any national curricular framework and asks questions like "why are the polar ice caps melting" or "how to build a space suit." The content was sourced from leading thinkers like NASA, Stanford University, UC Berkeley, Growing Leaders, UNESCO, and the World Economic Forum. All the content has been mapped back to all 17

SDGs and the OECD P21 Skills Framework. The incentivized learning model means that as girls explore activities that may ask them to watch a video, read an article, conduct an experiment or write a response, they win points. Once they build up their "rewards wallet" they can redeem their points for things like digital vouchers, mentoring sessions, work shadow opportunities, reading library access, or donating their points to a cause they care about.

The program was piloted for ten months across 7,000+ girls and 50 schools and not-for-profits in New Delhi, Seattle, and Atlanta. I was fortunate enough to lead the pilot in New Delhi with 6,000 participants. A deliberate decision was made to pilot the app across elite private, and affordable private and government schools in all three locations. The pilot was successful, with girls completing 90,000+ activity steps, winning 600+ rewards and donating 370,000 points (matched with a financial contribution from EY) to organizations such as Girls Who Code, AI for Good, and Junior Achievement. Girls also spent over one million minutes exploring content. The app also had a measured impact on the girls' STEM interest, expressed commitment (whether they'd continue with STEM learning), value (in the world around them), and competence (ability) as well as systems thinking, leadership, self-confidence, teamwork, and more. At its conclusion, the EY STEM Tribe pilot had been featured in the Nobel Prize Summit, the UN General Compact on Gender Equality, and in industry conferences. It was also recognized by the OECD as an Outstanding Public Sector Innovation and the International Center for Research on Women as a key initiative enabling livelihoods for women in India.

The entire pilot experience was an absolute thrill as somebody on the product and program side. For example, one morning, a group of girls at our very first government school were having trouble registering on the platform. They had never seen an "MMDDYY format form" before. I took this feedback to the engineers who changed the form that same day. Small changes like this showed us how fluid and dynamic a product can be once it reaches the end user. EY STEM app is an "inclusive" innovation at its core, with the team being driven by the objective of closing the gender gap in technology. The app generates no revenue and is free for all stakeholders. After the successful pilot in India, Seattle, and Atlanta, the teams have been working on Phase Two of the program, scaling the app to 100,000 girls across ten-plus countries. This gave us the opportunity to use learnings from the field and question the existing "inclusivity." While it was clearly impactful, in order to resonate with contexts around the world, would we not need to make changes to ensure impact for girls in Oceania, Southeast Asia, the Middle East, and the Americas?

We said yes, and started by ensuring that we prioritize underserved communities across our scaling locations and work to fit the app to local contexts. With the benefit of detailed insights from the app, we saw a higher learning impact from girls in schools further down the socio-economic ladder, and reached out to participants who would benefit the most from the platform. We also made nearly 60,000 changes to simplify the app's content and added subtitles, included videos from inspirational women changemakers across all ages in STEM, revised our rewards framework, and made user experience-driven changes. Finally, we began reaching out to leading STEM thinkers across our target regions – universities, individuals, foundations, and nonprofits. We are currently engaging to gamify their content into activities that can complement the existing content on the app.

In the spirit of inclusivity, we included the arts, so that our STEM aim became one of STEAM. Social and Emotional Learning, Race and Identity, Design Thinking and Individual Purpose will now feature prominently alongside the app's ever-changing content. We are continuing to partner with diverse content providers and bring this conversation to the forefront with every opportunity we get.

What makes this program powerful for me now is not necessarily the size of the effort, the awards or even the team. It's the endless effort to make it more inclusive. The aim is now around how this can help a wider group of girls and how each technical tweak can possibly make an impact. I've had the incredible opportunity to see how "tech for social good" isn't just an industry buzzword but something that can completely realign professional purpose.

After 100,000 girls are impacted by the app by June 2022, we will focus on ensuring its complete financial sustainability as well as its global reach. Until then, we will continue to deal with challenges head on – attitudes that an app on a phone can be anything except a distraction, our contribution towards increased "screen time" and the increased suspicion around EdTech after a rapid and unsustainable boom in places like India, for example. The strength of this innovation lies in its foundation – giving each bias, challenge, or criticism the dignity of the team's time and thinking regardless of where it came from. I'm proud that we are listening, thinking, and reacting in real time. It's knowing that we're working with and for the girls and potentially empowering them with knowledge and exposure.

The first time I felt I had the best job was going for a meeting in the corner office on the 12th floor of an office building in a suit. The first time I knew I had the best job in the world was my last session at a school huddled under a big guava tree, talking to 120 girls and sitting on the grass. It makes me smile every time I think about how many people will feel that same shift all over the world.

The COVID-19 pandemic and the future of inclusive innovation

The pandemic has magnified the impacts of unequal access to innovative employment, as well as underscoring the need for rapid, purpose-driven innovation in times of crisis. Thus, the need for innovation that benefits society, across demographic groups, industries, and geographic regions, has never been more urgent. The pandemic has also shown that innovation can – and does – come from all types of people and organizations. For example, a team of software developers that took part in the Hack Co Vy hackathon in Vietnam (see Box 3.3 for more details) adapted their last-mile delivery robot called Beetle Bot, featured in Box 5.2, in the COVID-19 pandemic so that it could help deliver medicine and medical supplies in hospitals that were trying to reduce human-to-human contact.

There is also greater awareness of the need for system design changes in order to further enable innovation to emanate from, and for, the benefit of the whole of society. The causes of underrepresentation are numerous, and include constraints on the supply of labor – such as insufficient training or desire to participate – which leads to a small set of initial applicants from underrepresented groups. And, of course, there are demand-side challenges, for example, conscious or subconscious preferences on the part of investors and employers that inhibit sufficient investment in, or employment of, applicants based upon demographic traits.

However, the pandemic has also ushered in an opportunity to draw lessons on which innovations, and broader approaches to innovation, are effective. In this way, it has served as a critical juncture – meaning an event that acts as a shock to the system – as it created the cognitive space for rethinking existing socioeconomic systems.[12] In many respects, the society-wide response to COVID-19 has democratized the notion of who is an innovator and what innovation should be designed by and for. For instance, teenagers developed innovative personal protective equipment, such as helmets that allowed the wearer to still scratch their head, and social innovators found ways to enable the distribution of resources, such as rice and face masks, that don't require physical person-to-person co-location.[13] COVID-19 has prompted a rethink of innovation, away from one that narrowly emphasizes Silicon Valley–style technological innovation and high-tech startups.

Furthermore, studies on lesson-learning in the context of the crisis have shown that efforts to institutionalize new processes in response to previous pandemics helped assuage the impact of COVID-19.[14] Research has also found that some technologies, such as AI, can help achieve broad economic growth, particularly the UN SDGs.[15] In the context of innovation, the pandemic has already been said to have shifted the thinking about innovation towards a more inclusive way, in terms of public sector agility, data governance, the role of civil society, grassroots innovators, and social innovators.

Box 5.2 Beetle Bot: adapting the direction of innovation in times of crisis

By Ida Uusikyla, UNDP Vietnam

After obtaining their degrees in computer science, a group of friends – Hien Nguyen, Hung Nguyen, Trieu Nguyen, and Quang Tran – were enthusiastic about setting up a company to put their newly acquired skills to test. They are a team of highly talented AI-Robotics scientists and blockchain engineers who have published in academic journals and wanted to apply their skills and knowledge to real-world applications. What brought the team together was their passion for researching and developing cutting-edge technologies to solve critical societal problems of today.

According to Quang Tran, one of the founders, "AIOZ is a DeepTech company, Researching and Developing (R&D) AI, Robotics & Blockchain technologies for next-gen content delivery, video analytics, mobile robotics systems, smart city, and beyond." In the early days, the team built several products, including optimal delivery scheduling, route optimization, warehouse management, and sales forecasting. The goal was to come up with a solution to be able to move things around easily; they felt that these "last-mile" logistics are critical for optimizing local commerce and increasing productivity and so wanted to innovate there. "The first online food order and delivery service was a pizza from Pizza Hut in 1994, since then, we have not seen a fundamental change in the way we do delivery," Quang said. Current delivery solutions such as Grab or Gojek Food delivery have their own limitations such as costs and efficiency, he continued. In the Fourth Industrial Revolution, we need to continue to accelerate automated delivery – so, the team says, now is the time to build and develop robots.

To achieve this, the team of software engineers soon realized that they needed additional people who understood hardware development. They needed experts on developing components such as processors, circuit boards, memory devices, networks, and routers to bring the robot alive. This is how Anh Nguyen joined the team as a robotics scientist who is now leading the robotics team. He joined because he found academics too theoretical, wanted a more grounded understanding of sustainable development. He sees AIOZ as a bridge to connect academic researchers to real-world industrial challenges. Now, four years later, the Singapore-based company has a team of over 30 people, including both software and hardware engineers focused exclusively on AI, robotics, and blockchain in solving critical societal problems.

The development of the first robot started in 2019. It was developed for last-mile food delivery, similar to Grab Food, but as their autonomous robot cousin. The team's vision was to change food and package delivery through the application of advancing AI and Robotics technologies. Then the global COVID-19 pandemic broke out. Something no one was expecting at the time. Quang, Anh, and the team, however, were quick to respond in the fight against COVID-19, for which Vietnam soon became famous.

Particularly, technology has played a crucial role in keeping Vietnam functional during various lockdowns and quarantines. The pandemic opened up new opportunities and markets for healthcare-related solutions. In particular, the AIOZ team realized the potential of autonomous robots for hospitals treating COVID-19 patients and turned the prototype they had developed into a service robot assisting doctors in the hospital. Robotic technologies would significantly help safely reduce the burden on Vietnamese doctors and healthcare workers who have been taking care of hundreds of patients and thousands of people under quarantine. With this idea, the Beetle Bot was born.

The team wanted to create a bigger impact with their innovation, so they entered – and won – the "Hack Co Vy" organized by UNDP Vietnam, AngelHack, and Hanoi Youth Union in April 2020. From this hackathon, Beetle Bot was developed with the mission of being a helpful assistant to reduce the risks of these frontline workers being exposed to the virus, helping them to stay safe in order to contribute their best to the fight against the pandemic.

Ever since Spring 2020, the team has been iterating and adapting the solution to be suitable for the healthcare sector. Prototype testing revealed that they needed to better balance between cost and functionality. To illustrate the tension, early feedback showed that carrying heavy food and other equipment requires a strong motor, but the strong motor means that the robot makes a lot of noise. This noise issue – the team learned – is a very important concern to doctors and nurses. It was so important, in fact, that the staff wanted to treat the COVID-19 patients themselves rather than rely on the noisy support of the Beetle Bot. This was an unexpected insight.

The team rolled up their sleeves and got to work developing a better robot for hospital use. It needed to be cost effective, strong, and quiet. The cost of development was very high. This was because the hardware was costly as the team had to experiment through lots of trial and error to come up with a complete solution. Also, software development took a lot of time and effort in R&D. One of the main technical challenges apart from the noisy motor remained the issue of making the robot fully autonomous, which has taken the team over two years to solve. The delivery function is very useful but only when it's fully autonomous. To address this, the team has been working to remove redundant parts and optimize the design so the motor slows down and makes less noise. Now the new robot moves very smoothly, and crucially, quietly.

"In the beginning we made many mistakes – we came up with the product ourselves because we found it useful but to make it actually usable in the hospital setting, it's important to understand the end-user demands," Quang said. "Some of the features we initially thought were important, were not very useful in the end. Multiple functions including disinfection and video were too much," he shared. In this case, the team adopted the mantra that "less is more." They realized that the most important thing was to understand the demands of the end users. "We learned this through a lot of surveys, discussions with the team, and many different mockups," Quang shared. Some of this feedback they got through UNDP-hosted webinars that connected the hospitals and development teams in aiming to strengthen the ecosystem of robotic developers for health. The team then spent nearly a full week in the hospital to deploy the robot and discuss the opportunities and challenges with the doctors and nurses in the field.

Overall, COVID-19 didn't change the long-term vision for the AIOZ team, but opened up new opportunities – the hospital delivery robot being just one use-case. The team, however, is more determined than ever to use their knowledge and expertise in robotics and AI to address sustainable development challenges. The long-term vision for the Beetle Bot is to add more features so it can work in other settings such as restaurants, airports, or universities. Since the key function of the robot is delivery, its use can be applied to multiple sectors. "To adapt it for other specific sectors, we need to do more research, especially further discussion with the new clients as every sector is different," Quang explained. "For instance, medication delivery is different from food. We need to make the robot safe and clean and customize based on end-user needs," he continued. Overall, the value proposition for the product is a "low-cost solution to reduce manual work for humans." Automation of manual work holds a huge opportunity to boost productivity, efficiency, and competitiveness which are the front and center of Vietnam's economic development. "We see a bright future of robotic applications in healthcare in the form of delivery robots in hospitals or service robots for taking care of the elderly," Quang says.

Policy strategies for the future of inclusive innovation

Focusing on the bridging of policy, theory, and practice of inclusive innovation, we suggest ways in which governments, in particular, can build on and strengthen approach.

1. Coordinate cross-government action towards inclusive innovation

Innovation promotion tends to be the responsibility of ministries or departments that oversee science and technology policies or economic and industrial development. These departments often prioritize supporting the development of new technologies and building up regions, sectors, and firms that already have high economic growth potential. Meanwhile, responsibility for questions relating to inequality, poverty, and social growth tends to sit within ministries of social affairs. Cross-fertilization of ideas and solutions between these areas could be a powerful stimulus for inclusive forms of innovation, to orient towards solving environmental and social challenges, and to think of innovation beyond a high-tech sense. However, the mechanisms to allow for collaboration across government in these areas are often underdeveloped or lacking.

In the Philippines, the government has tried to address this challenge by framing the country's innovation law as an Inclusive Innovation Industrial Strategy. Government stakeholders told us that the new law's intention is to make the Filipino innovation system more cohesive and to ensure that science, technology, and innovation policies promote social inclusion, as well as technological invention.[16] Within the Philippines, the National Economic Development Authority has been tasked with creating a cross-government National Innovation Council, which will bring together all the main government departments with innovation responsibilities to increase R&D in both high-value sectors and to address social challenges – particularly those that affect low-income groups.

2. Tailor innovation support models to local needs

There is enormous pressure to build local Silicon Valley–styled ecosystems. Such clusters promise a panacea: to advance disruptive innovation, which in turn boosts productivity and spurs job growth. In order to do so, policymakers may study which policies have been pursued in the Valley, or more proximate innovation clusters. However, copying what has worked elsewhere is unlikely to prove effective locally, if initiatives are not tailored to fit the local economic conditions, social values, and needs of a country's government and its people. The innovator responsible for the Rice ATM offers a vivid example of the role of a context-relevant solution to a challenge faced in urban Vietnam during the COVID-19 pandemic, as detailed in Box 5.3.

Multi-stakeholder dialogue processes can advance a shared understanding of inclusive innovation, one that goes beyond seeing innovation as synonymous with technological advance and explores structural impediments, such as education, to wider society's participation in innovation. For example, a workshop organized by the UNDP in Hanoi in December 2019 brought together government policymakers from multiple ministries, union representatives, and researchers to define inclusive innovation policy in the

Box 5.3 Rice ATM: innovation to bring people together, without transmitting COVID-19

By Berlin Tran, Lecturer at the University of Economics Ho Chi Minh City

> I saw that there were thousands of people wanting to do charity, and there were thousands in need of essential food.

In 2020, around five million workers across Vietnam struggled without income due to the fallout of COVID-19. The situation was especially dire for the informally employed and low-income laborers, workers without contracts, and youth and elderly workers, many of whom lost income overnight when strict measures like social distancing and lockdown were implemented. Their families could no longer afford even the most essential thing – food. At the same time, philanthropists were lost as to how they could give out food to the poor without creating a crowd and potentially a viral hotbed. This dilemma was noticed by Hoang Tuan Anh, an engineer and businessman in Ho Chi Minh City.

Mr. Hoang pieced together the simple technologies his company possessed to create a semiautomatic rice dispenser, which he called Rice ATM, to connect support givers and recipients.

Mr. Hoang is a mechanical and electrical engineer and runs a company, called Blue Universe, that distributes electronic locks and designs solutions for smart homes. When social distancing and lockdown were implemented nationwide in 2020, he saw that, with widespread and sudden redundancies, not only informal workers but even a "typical [Vietnamese] salaryman" might not be able to afford "daily meals" for oneself and his/her family. Moreover, he was able to witness firsthand the socioeconomic fallout of COVID-19 among the poor, since his shop was located in one of the less affluent districts of Ho Chi Minh City. At the same time, Mr. Hoang noticed that the philanthropy community was "[at a] loss with COVID," even though it had always been quick to volunteer and make charitable donations during crises:

> We have a national spirit, a strong sharing and giving spirit, [but] the Government called for not crowding, and any charity work might create a crowd, then a viral hotbed, so everyone was concerned and nobody knew how to help others.

Thus, the engineer discovered a key problem caused by the pandemic in Vietnam – a lack of "means to connect support givers and recipients." This motivated him to develop a solution.

His solution was a semiautomatic dispenser of rice, called Rice ATM. The machine comprised a human-sized box (like an ATM) and a rice container, which were pieced together with the technologies and machineries he had around the shop, including an electronic lock with camera, a water tank (to contain rice), and a lock-testing machine repurposed into a flow controller for outgoing rice. To use the ATM, a person first presses a button on the box, which turns on the electronic lock, which is also installed; the lock then sends video feed to an operator working remotely who, with a smartphone, can then see the person coming for rice and control the ATM to release it. Mr. Hoang engineered the ATM in a way that it could run 24/7 and dispense rice at a rate of five to ten packets per minute, each weighing 1.5kg–2kg. The first ATM was installed in front of his shop, dispensing rice donated by friends and family. Hand sanitizers were also provided, and there were drawings on the ground to help users queue at two meters apart; a member of staff, including Mr. Hoang himself, was always present for assistance.

The Rice ATM addressed multiple issues at the same time. To begin with, there was no physical interaction between rice donors and recipients, and in fact donors could send rice and recipients could come and use the ATM at any time. Neither did recipients need to crowd or fight over the rice, as Mr. Hoang had engineered the ATM to be fast and always operational:

> Normally the mentality is that people crowd because they don't want to lose their portion. I tried to change this way of thinking by letting the ATMs run 24/7, and rice was never depleted, so no one had to crowd or wrestle for a portion, they could come anytime, midnight was okay, 1 or 2am was okay, so they would not feel missing out.

Fairness was also ensured, in that the ATM video recorded who had received rice during the day, so if the same person came multiple times, the remote operator could control the machine to not release rice. This had the added perk of preventing quarrel: "As givers it is hard for us to refuse them, and this can cause quarrels. But a machine can refuse." Finally, the ATM was a scalable solution, being small enough to transport in a minivan and simple enough to be installed in the streets and operated by anyone with a smartphone.

The very first ATM went viral on social media after Mr. Hoang showed it on Facebook to call for rice donation, and shortly afterwards the mainstream media picked up on the story. Thanks to such coverage, he received "tons more rice" from philanthropists and managed to offer his solution to various provinces across Vietnam for free. In the end, he made over 100 ATMs, 30 of which were gifted to the government, and the amount of rice dispensed was approximately 10,000 tons, worth around US$5 million. Perhaps most importantly, the engineer made his design an open intellectual property by letting news channels and content creators on social media film the inner workings of the machine, as well as how he himself conducted the operations (e.g. loading rice, managing queues). Speaking about his contribution to Vietnam's response to the pandemic, he humbly said:

> My role was very small. What was important was that I could connect people who were willing to help with people who needed help. Hence, we created this butterfly effect.

Since the first Rice ATM, many people were inspired, and different versions of the machine were created to adapt to different contexts. For instance, one adaptation was a nonelectric ATM that could be operated with a foot pedal, thus suitable for rural and mountainous areas where there are shortages of electricity. Looking ahead, Mr. Hoang's intention is for the government to continue using the rice ATMs to help the vulnerable, especially during other pandemics or natural disasters. Through the Ministry of Foreign Affairs, he sent some ATMs to Cambodia, India, Myanmar, the Philippines, and Timor-Leste. For Mr. Hoang, the most important thing is that "when people face difficulties, rice still flows from the ATMs to their rice cooker."

local Vietnamese context.[17] Participants explored which international models could be relevant, as well as how existing local policy efforts could be adapted to better drive innovation that delivers economic and social benefits. One of the key takeaways was that innovation is currently too narrowly understood in relation to science and technology policy; efforts need to be taken to advance an understanding of innovation that is in line with Schumpeter: that of a novel product or process that stands to boost productivity, not necessarily an information and communications technology.

3. More inclusive policymaking processes

A key observation from our field research is that there are emerging efforts to involve those who stand to benefit in policy design and governance. Without such participation, inclusive innovation policymaking poses the risk of creating a system where people are innovated for, but where they have little agency to represent themselves as problem-solvers. To deliver a positive impact, the policymaking process needs to begin with giving a voice to those who are impacted, to ensure that efforts are "by, for, and of" society, rather than emanating from elsewhere.[18] The policymaking process should be informed by the mantra that the problem-owners should also be the problem-solvers.

What is shaping the future of inclusive innovation?

Our research found a clear interest on the part of government policymakers and other actors in the ASEAN region to use innovation as a means of addressing societal and environmental challenges and bringing more people, places, and sectors into innovation ecosystems. But we also observed a general lack of coordination within governments on this agenda, and a disconnect between what is happening inside and outside government. Many of the socially-oriented tech startups we spoke to in the region felt like they were operating without the funding, policies, and regulations required to really develop or scale up their solutions.

Our research team conducted a horizon scan in June and July 2021 by canvassing social media (Facebook, Twitter, and Instagram), blog posts (e.g. Medium), and news sources (national and key newspapers in each country and across the region). We also looked at Google Trends, to see what was trending, and completed a keyword search on Medium, searching for keywords and for a given year (e.g. 2021). The keyword strings used were similar to those that we used to identify inclusion innovation content and trends more broadly for the study. The difference here was that we covered a broader and different set of sources: social media, news, and press releases rather than published books, articles, and policies. The aim of the exercise was to find what is on the horizon but is not yet obvious.

The horizon scanning was completed across a few steps. After the keyword search, the research team used Miro – a collaborative online platform for sharing ideas and stories – prompts to pull together examples, links, images, etc. Then we conducted a Miro-based session to assess themes and codify the signals (as weak or strong) and the drivers and trends. We are aware that these themes are not wholly new, but in our scanning, we see them as rapidly emerging towards the mainstream of policy and practice. Here we highlight the three emerging themes most evidenced in the variety of traditional and social media sources we analyzed: sustainability, digitalization, and financial inclusion.

Sustainability

Policies geared towards sustainability, in both the government and corporate world, have been on the uptick lately in Southeast Asia. Policies intended to propel sustainability are guided by a few factors across the region. First of all, COVID-19 has served as a critical juncture, giving the world an opportunity to reevaluate our unsustainable relationship with the planet. More awareness regarding resource exploitation has emerged, as seen with the UNDP and the Swiss State Secretariat for Economic Affairs partnership to foster sustainability in Indonesian palm oil production.[19] Similarly, in Vietnam, the MPI aims to raise investment and resources in advanced technologies for green growth and more efficiently use natural resources. Efforts have been growing since the country adopted the five-year Vietnam Country Planning Framework in 2016.[20] Since the onset of COVID-19, sustainable tourism is being pursued at a greater rate, with policymakers presenting this type of tourism, which is respectful to local heritage and protects the environment, as a form of green growth.[21]

Digitalization

There are policies indicating that digitizing the future of the workforce is on its way. For instance, in May 2020, the Philippines Department of Science and Technology (DOST) launched the Science for Change program (S4CP) to accelerate the use of technological innovation in Filipino businesses.[22] Under the program, the aim is to have the innovation capacity of the Philippines levelled up by introducing new technologies, and new machinery, to Filipino businesses. In addition to wider industrial inclusion efforts, awareness of demographic differences in participation rates is growing. For instance, women in the Philippines are increasingly involved in digital workspaces, in recognition of their historically low rates of participation and the opportunity for change, as presented by COVID-19.[23] Policies are, collectively, striving to help local businesses to harness the latest digital developments and technology, and purposefully increase the rates of participation of underrepresented groups.

Looking at the demand side of the market for entrepreneurs, while e-commerce was already prevalent, the pandemic catalyzed a major rise. For businesses, e-commerce has been a means to reach customers under lockdowns, or those who are less keen to shop as normal. By moving online (small) businesses avoid the costs associated with volatilities in inflows of customers and can open and close businesses at the whim of restrictions.

Financial inclusion

Southeast Asia is home to one of the world's largest unbanked populations. According to a study by KPMG, as of 2018, only 27 percent of those living in Southeast Asia had a bank account.[24] This leaves a huge gap in banking penetration, with around 438 million unbanked individuals. In poorer countries such as Cambodia, where the figure is 5 percent, the numbers are even lower. Lacking access to financial services has created barriers to escape poverty as it is difficult to have savings or borrow money without bank access.[25] This problem can be translated into opportunities for services such as mobile financial services or other financial products leveraging digital platforms and technologies.

Policies are strengthening around the aim of growing financial inclusion. With the pandemic sprang an onslaught of new businesses being established and operated from home and therefore many people in need of financial products and services to effectively run their companies. Women-led businesses have, in particular, received support given this shift. In Indonesia, the Ministry of Women Empowerment and Child Protection is providing training and digital literacy courses to women who own micro businesses.[26] In a similar vein, the initiative Rebuilding Better: Fostering Business Resilience Post-COVID-19 – launched by the International Labour Organization (ILO) and the JPMorgan Chase Foundation in February 2021 – aims to help women entrepreneurs by leveraging digital tools to access critical support services, such as financial resources, training, market information, and networks.[27] More generally, financial inclusion is also being observed with the expansion of fintech to underserved populations. This trend can be observed in the Philippines where Bangko Sentral ng Pilipinas is launching several programs, such as providing 70 million free national IDs to make banking more accessible.[28]

While these emerging forms offer promise, the risk of "inclusive innovation washing" is something to worry about. As one of our advisors lamented, if inclusive innovation includes everything, then it means nothing. In this book we have worked to build a bridge between policy and practice, and in the language used by those doing inclusive innovation, and those researching it. What we did not include were activities or products that were either not new or novel, and so, not innovative. We also did not profile innovations that did not have environmental or social challenges central to their motivation. We hope that by drawing a line around what inclusive innovation is, we are better able to avoid the risk of it becoming a "washing" term.

A call to action for the future of inclusive innovation

Though much of what we have covered in this book has been current to the early 2020s, we close by underscoring that while inclusive innovation as a term is relatively new, the underlying idea is not. The notion of supporting technological innovation for social and environmental benefit for the local context began with the AT movement in the 1950s. The movement was asserted as a strategy to assuage the tendency towards innovation investments in – and the gains being captured by – the rich, industrialized world.[29] In emerging economy contexts, AT emphasized the promotion of locally-relevant technological capabilities and minimal environmental damage.

The particular language of inclusive innovation came, as mentioned in Chapter 1, when Mark Dutz coined the phrase in a 2007 World Bank report on sustainable innovation in India. He defined it as "knowledge creation and absorption efforts that are most relevant to the needs of the poor."[30] Shortly after the term appeared, inclusive innovation was invoked by practitioners, academia, and policymakers. The concept has grown in use in recent years, and is often associated with the BoP consumers or participation in technology-centric innovation. In the contemporary use of the term inclusive innovation, technology has become synonymous with ICT and inclusion focusing primarily on social issues. A richer understanding of technology as a novel tool has been lost. And, the environmental degradation issues that were central to the AT movement have fallen by the wayside.

Our call for action is to reinstate an understanding of innovation that includes social forms, such as the Zero Baht Shop, and the Circular Design Lab, and a wider range of technologies, as in the Rice ATM, SJI, and Proximity Designs examples profiled in this book. Tech for environmental and social good – as epitomized by DMap, Learning Coin, and the EY STEM app – is part of inclusive innovation, but is not the only way. Multiple stakeholders can come together in new ways, as in FemLab.Co, and innovations can include new low-tech products, such as ABC Bakery's "pink bakery movement," to simultaneously address both environmental and social challenges and to link urban and rural populations effectively.

It is clear that there is growing momentum and opportunity for inclusive innovation to drive substantive societal and environmental impact in Southeast Asia and beyond. Throughout the book we have revealed how a range of actors – including academia, civil society, funders and investors, governments and international organizations, grassroots innovators, large firms, startups, and SMEs – are advancing innovation that has environmental and societal aims at the heart. Policymakers and practitioners alike are aware of the myriad causes and consequences of exclusion, and so approach innovation in order to benefit wider society, to drive equity, and advance regenerative futures. The risk, though, is that efforts continue to take a narrow view of innovation and inclusion.

Now is the time for inclusive innovation's theory, policy, and practice to come together, so that the term does not come to be used disingenuously, nor used in too restrictive a way. For instance, in *The Dark Side of Social Enterprises*, it is argued that it is important to look beyond "the myth of impact" and to be open to the fact that enterprises could be "corrupted by conflicting motives and the pursuit of private gain."[31] There are also critical development frameworks that strive to go post-development, by taking a human-centered, pluralistic approach.[32] Inclusive innovation is not a panacea, as these critiques rightly note. But, orienting towards addressing intersectional environmental and social challenges through a variety of innovation paths, as we have shown in this book, is a promising alternative. More of society can be empowered to innovate in response to environmental and social challenges they are experiencing in their local context.

We close with our Call to Action. Academics, policymakers, and practitioners can come together to take forward an understanding and practice of inclusive innovation that sees problem-owners as problem-solvers, environmental challenges as central, and innovation as wider than ICT. Join us on LinkedIn at the #InclusiveInnovation Community of Practice. Share your story, and connect with others active in the space. Let's together advance research, dialogue about what works, and what doesn't, in terms of innovation that has environmental and societal aims at the heart.

Notes

1 UN, Human Development Report (2020), The next frontier: human development and the Anthropocene.
2 Including Heeks, Foster, and Nugroho, "New models of inclusive innovation for development"; Zehavi and Breznitz, "Distribution-sensitive innovation policies"; Klingler-Vidra, *Global Review of Diversity and Inclusion in Business Innovation*; Glennie, Ollard, Stanley, and Klingler-Vidra, "Strategies for Supporting Inclusive Innovation."
3 Heeks, Foster, and Nugroho, "New models of inclusive innovation for development"; Zehavi and Breznitz, "Distribution-sensitive innovation policies."
4 Glennie, Ollard, Stanley, and Klingler-Vidra, *Strategies for Supporting Inclusive Innovation.*
5 Cozzens and Thakur, *Innovation and Inequality.*
6 Planes-Satorra and Paunov, "Inclusive innovation policies."
7 Planes-Satorra and Paunov, "Inclusive innovation policies."
8 Zehavi and Breznitz, "Distribution-sensitive innovation policies."
9 Klingler-Vidra, *Global Review of Diversity and Inclusion in Business Innovation.*
10 Stanley, Glennie, and Gabriel, "How inclusive is innovation policy?"
11 Zehavi and Breznitz, "Distribution-sensitive innovation policies."
12 Charles Leadbeater, "Innovation and crisis: is our fight against COVID-19 a critical juncture?" *Nesta.* December 9, 2020. www.nesta.org.uk/blog/innovation-and-crisis-our-fight-against-COVID-19-critical-juncture/.
13 Berlin Tran and Robyn Klingler-Vidra, "Good news stories from Vietnam's second wave – involving dragon fruit burgers and mask ATMs." *The Conversation.* September 17, 2020. https://theconversation.com/good-news-stories-from-vietnams-second-wave-involving-dragon-fruit-burgers-and-mask-atms-145940.
14 Ramon Pacheco Pardo, *Preventing the Next Pandemic: Lessons from East Asia* (London: King's College London, 2020).
15 Ricardo Vinuesa, Hossein Azizpour, Iolanda Leite, Madeline Balaam, Virginia Dignum, Sami Domisch, Anna Felländer, Simone Daniela Langhans, Max Tegmark, and Francesco Fuso Nerini, "The role of artificial intelligence in achieving the Sustainable Development Goals." *Nature Communications* 11, no. 233 (2020).
16 See also Klingler-Vidra and Lor, "Bringing the environment back into our Understanding of Inclusive Innovation."
17 UNDP Vietnam, *Inclusive Innovation Policy for the Next Development Stage in Vietnam.*
18 UNDP Vietnam, *Inclusive Innovation Policy for the Next Development Stage in Vietnam.*
19 SECO, "Fostering sustainability in the Indonesian palm oil production." February 2, 2021. www.seco-cooperation.admin.ch/secocoop/en/home/laender/indonesia/palm_oil.html.

20 MPI, "Promotion of the MPI – GGGI partnership." September 8, 2017. www. mpi.gov.vn/en/Pages/tinbai.aspx?idTin=38120&idcm=133.

21 See, for example, Cade, 2021 regarding sustainable tourism in Phong Nha in Vietnam. Lynda Cade, "Could Phong Nha be one of Vietnam's top sustainable travel destinations?" *Sagoneer.* May 28, 2021. https://saigoneer.com/vietnam-tra vel/20338-could-phong-nha-be-one-of-vietnam-s-top-sustainable-travel-desti nations.

22 DOST, "DOST science for change program." May 5, 2020. www.dost.gov.ph/ 9-programs-and-projects/1811-dost-science-for-change-program.html#:~:text= Theper%20cent20Scienceper%20cent20forper%20cent20Changeper%20 cent20Program,andper%20cent20innovationper%20cent20areper%20 cent20gameper%20cent20changers.

23 Ana Kujundzic and Janneke Pieters, "Gender differences in automation risk in developing country labor markets." *Future of Work in the Global South.* July 2021. https://fowigs.net/gender-differences-in-automation-risk-in-developing-country-labor-markets/.

24 ASEAN Post, "Banking Southeast Asia's unbanked." January 1, 2019. https:// theaseanpost.com/article/banking-southeast-asias-unbanked-0.

25 Geoffrey Prentice, "A panacea for the unbanked in S-E Asia." *The Business Times.* April 23, 2019. www.businesstimes.com.sg/opinion/a-panacea-for-the-unbanked-in-s-e-asia.

26 Nina A. Loasana, "Indonesia, UK team up to launch training program for women entrepreneurs." *Jakarta Post.* November 11, 2020. www.thejakartapost.com/ news/2020/11/11/indonesia-uk-team-up-to-launch-training-program-for-women-entrepreneurs.html.

27 ILO, "The ILO and JPMorgan Chase Foundation join forces to support women entrepreneurs impacted by COVID-19." February 2, 2021. www.ilo.org/asia/ media-centre/news/WCMS_767793/lang--en/index.htm.

28 Mayvelin U. Caraballo, "BSP aims to print 70M national ID cards by year end." March 19, 2021. www.manilatimes.net/2021/03/19/business/business-top/bsp-aims-to-print-70m-national-id-cards-by-yearend/853055.

29 Jequier, *Appropriate Technology*; Kaplinsky, "Schumacher meets Schumpeter."

30 Dutz, *Unleashing India's Innovation*, xv.

31 Tina Dacin, "The dark side of social enterprises." *Smith School of Business.* December 16, 2013. http://qsb.ca/insight/videos/the_dark_side_of_social_enterpri ses. Others go even further, saying that social enterprises are not fit for purpose as they lack the scale to drive substantive change, and do not strive to solve the roots of the problems that they say they aim to address. Similarly, the literature also explores the lack of results intended to alleviate societal problems, whether that be through inclusive programs or resource-constrained NGOs. For more, see Belinda Bell, "Taking care of business: has social enterprise proved it is not fit for purpose?" *RSA Journal,* 5586, no. 3 (2021): 36–40.

32 Kothari, Salleh, Escobar, Demaria, and Acosta, *Pluriverse.*

Index

Note: Tables are in **bold** type and figures in *italics*. Endnotes are indicated by "n" and the endnote number after the page number e.g., 24n20 refers to endnote number 20 on page 24.